The Bizarre Story of *Guess v. Jordache* —Glamour, Greed, and Dirty Tricks in the Fashion Industry

by Christopher Byron

Simon & Schuster

New York London Toronto Sydney Tokyo Singapore

SIMON & SCHUSTER
Simon & Schuster Building
Rockefeller Center
1230 Avenue of the Americas
New York, New York 10020

Designed by Karolina Harris
Manufactured in the United States of America

10 9 8 7 6 5 4 3 2 1

Library of Congress Cataloging-in-Publication Data
Byron, Christopher.
   Skin tight: the bizarre story of Guess v. Jordache—glamour, greed,
and dirty tricks in the fashion industry/by Christopher Byron.
      p.   cm.
   Includes bibliographical references and index.
   1. Guess (Firm)—Trials, litigation, etc.   2. Jordache (Firm)—
Trials, litigation, etc.   3. Trials (Fraud)—California—Los Angeles.
4. Clothing trade—United States—Corrupt practices.   I. Title.
KF228.G84B97   1992
345.73′0263—dc20
[347.305263]   91-45465   CIP
ISBN 0-671-69475-8

For Katherine, who never stopped smiling.

Sin has many tools, but a lie is the handle whi
—OLIVER WENDF

Whoever lies down to sleep with a dog, gets
—*A Treasury of Jew*

Introduction

THIS is a story of vengeance and emotional violence in one of the roughest, nastiest business fights ever. Its battleground stretched from the garment district of New York, to the canyons of Beverly Hills, to the glare of television klieg lights in a committee room of Congress—but its roots traced back centuries into the hate-filled passions of North Africa and the Middle East.

To tell this story has been difficult on several levels, not least because of the extraordinary complexity of the case and the colossal public record created by the parties. The public record—found in archives from Hong Kong to Tel Aviv and dozens of points in between—became the primary source material for the book. The record includes the complete 5,000-page trial transcript in the matter of *Marciano v. Nakash,* Superior Court of the State of California, County of Los Angeles, No. C 524 347. I have also made use of copies of four volumes of memoranda and exhibits in the files of the Major Crimes Unit, U.S. Attorney's Office for the Southern District of New York. I have also drawn upon four volumes of transcripts of Guess Inc. board of directors meetings, as well as copies of approximately fifty hours of surreptitiously tape-recorded conversations released by the parties in various discovery proceedings.

I have also obtained copies of relevant memoranda and correspondence from the Public Prosecutor of Paris, Anti-Terrorist Division, and have likewise obtained, digested and made use of copies of all significant pleadings, motions and memoranda in the controversy. The preliminary and final reports of the House Committee on Government Operations' investigation into *Misconduct by Senior Managers in the Internal Revenue Service* have also been used extensively.

Fifty-three individuals involved in the controversy have been interviewed as well, many at great length. Wherever possible, quoted dialogue is derived from contemporaneous written memoranda, sworn depositions, and court testimony of the events in question. Where conflicts have arisen, I have pointed them out as well as discussed them in the chapter notes, which I urge the reader to review for the finer points of the story.

The research and writing of this book has ultimately spanned more than four years. At times the work has been a labor of love, at other times, one of pain and personal sadness. Through it all my extraordinary wife, Maria, has stood fast, once again offering the selfless support that makes authorship possible. I would also like to thank my marvelous agent, Victoria Pryor, whose representational skills are exceeded only by her capacities as an editor—which come free of charge for those lucky enough to work with her.

A number of other people also played important roles in the evolution of this book. In that regard, I'd like to thank Mr. Bob Bender, my editor at Simon & Schuster, who devoted a great deal of time and effort to helping me shape the manuscript; Ms. Linda P. Lerman, bibliographer of the Judaica studies archive at Yale University in New Haven, Connecticut, who opened the way into a field of scholarship I would never have been able to approach without her; Mr. David Newberg, who made possible a key interview at a critical moment; and Mr. Jeremy Nussbaum, for the insightful legal and editorial advice he rendered. I would also especially like to thank Mr. Edward Kosner, the editor of *New York* magazine, whose support and encouragement as I labored with this book never wavered once.

Christopher Byron
Weston, Connecticut
1991

PART ONE

Chapter 1

At the start of the twentieth century, rare was the civilized European who set foot in the Mediterranean port of Tripoli—and for good reason. From the sea, Tripoli would have seemed a city of Oriental splendors, its minarets and spires set magically against the pale North African sky. But closer inspection would have revealed a place of almost unimaginable squalor, with narrow and twisting streets teeming with Arabs, Berbers, Jews, Maltese, Greeks, and Italians. In the whole of Tripoli, a city of fifty thousand, the visitor could have walked upon but a handful of paved streets. There would have been no lights or indoor plumbing, nor even much in the way of a local government. Civil rule—such as it was—resided in the hands of a Turkish pasha who cared little for the violence and disease that lurked beyond his garden walls.

In the air of Tripoli would have been scents heavy and strange to European nostrils—orange blossoms and spice, date palms and saffron. The smell of farina cakes frying in oil, or couscous, would have clung to the courtyards, mixed with the sour odor of lambs' heads and donkey feet roasting on spits. The visitor's tongue would have burned day and night from consuming Libyan red peppers in almost every dish served.

In the year 1909, a young French scholar of Hebrew history, Nahum Slouschz, chose to venture into this world. Hoping eventually to publish the results, Slouschz had undertaken a challenge that had lured historians and adventurers throughout the ages: to search for the lost tribes of Israel.

In Slouschz's case, the specific focus of his assignment was daunting: to research the ethnography of the Sephardic diaspora to North Africa, which came as the climax to the Spanish Inquisition. To escape persecution, some Sephardim had sailed for Italy, and others had departed for Greece and the Holy Land. Still others had fled southward across the Mediterranean to the coastal cities of North Africa.

Once ashore in Africa, many found welcome, but in some cities rapes and assaults were common. Cut off from their homeland, the wandering Sephardim began by and by to drift southward, to Rabat and Casablanca, to Marrakech and Fez. Eventually, they became no more than a memory, as the North African interior swallowed them in its vast and empty embrace.

Where had they gone? What had happened in the five hundred years that had followed? Answers were all but nonexistent, and when travelers did venture forth, they returned with observations hopelessly inadequate to the scope of the mystery. In 1790, a Hebrew-speaking Jew from Lombardy, Samuel Romanelli, journeyed to Morocco and came back with the following observation: "The Jews stand when urinating, while the Arabs squat."

Standing or squatting, these were the people Nahum Slouschz had gone in search of. And the questions he hoped to answer went far beyond their bathroom habits. After thirty generations amidst Arabs and Berbers, would the Sephardic Jews from Spain still even think of themselves as Jews at all?

At the beginning of the twentieth century, North Africa was a land with few roads and almost no rail connections—and nothing whatsoever in the way of what European society would have regarded as civilization. Within the walls of Morocco's fortified cities were the customs and folkways of another age—harems and slaves, blood feuds and superstitions. One English traveler of the late nineteenth century returned to London from Morocco to write, "I have seen England in the Middle Ages."

Outside the walls of the cities, the countryside teemed with brigands and thieves. A French explorer, upon returning to Europe, is reported to have remarked that any fair-minded application of the Islamic punishment of hand amputation for thievery would render Morocco a nation of cripples.

Yet deeper and deeper into the interior Slouschz went, from the Jewish colonies of Tripoli and Tunis into the mountainous and sandy wastes that spread southward toward Waidi and Timbuctoo—an area known vaguely in Europe as "Negroland." Wild bands of Tuaregs lurked in the bush, and at one point Slouschz fell ill from the food and climate and nearly died.

But still he kept on, as the continent opened before him, an endless expanse of poisoned waterholes and marauding, bloodthirsty Berbers. It was an expedition of danger at every turn, made all the worse by French colonial politics, which had lately stirred up guerrilla warfare throughout the region. The problem traced back to a seventy-year-old incident in which the dey of Algiers lost his temper in a quarrel and struck the French consul with a fly swatter. In response, France sent its army to avenge the insult by conquering Algeria, and was now trying to take over Morocco as well. In many places, who ruled—the Turks, the French, the Berbers, the Arabs—was a matter of some dispute.

Yet as his precarious adventure continued, Slouschz eventually began to hear stories about a place hidden away from strife and time itself, somewhere high in the upper valleys of the Atlas Mountains, where Morocco meets the desert. The village was called Debdu, and it was here, legend had it, that many of the Andalusian Sephardim had settled. The village sat astride what had apparently once been an established trade route into the interior—with indigo, hashish, and contraband rifles moving north to Europe from the wild southern "Dra'a" country, and barter wares and provisions moving south for the caravans departing from Marrakech and Rabat. Five hundred years had passed since Jews had first set foot in Debdu, and they were by now said to outnumber the Arabs and Berbers almost two to one.

According to accounts, Debdu was at once fertile and isolated, its two thousand inhabitants cut off from the world by spectacular, vaulting cliffs of bright yellow rock all around. Over the cliffs streamed icy cascades of water, pouring down silver on silver from the snow-covered peaks above the clouds. A thousand feet below sat the village, with its rose-colored cottages opening on to a valley of meadows and wild flowers.

In the year 1788, a Reverend Dr. M. Edrehi of Cambridge University had journeyed into the interior of Morocco, and forty-five years later he published Europe's first known reference—albeit a brief and perplexing one—to life in the mysterious mountain village. In a work entitled *An Historical Account of the Ten Tribes,* he had written, "There is a peculiar and very great wonder in the kingdom of Morocco in Africa. There is a town in that country, built on a very high mountain; the name of the town is called Dobdo."

Though the manuscript had failed to enlighten the reader about what Debdu's "peculiar and very great wonder" actually was, it did describe the village as enjoying "a fine climate and a beautiful air . . . [and] a great many fine gardens."

A century later, a French explorer had happened upon the place. He too had been taken by Debdu's physical charms and had written, "No words can convey the freshness of the scene."

Yet scarcely had Slouschz himself arrived than he began to detect something else. In his journal, Slouschz noted that Debdu's inhabitants wore the beards and black caftans of Sephardim and belonged, moreover, "to the handsome, Spanish type." Yet there was something else. Exactly what it was, Slouschz couldn't say—a kind of vague tension in the air.

In his chronicle of nearly a century and a half earlier, the Reverend Dr. Edrehi of Cambridge had remarked upon the fact that the inhabitants of Debdu appeared to be surprisingly aggressive—indeed, even warlike—in their otherwise tranquil world. Among other things, they had apparently developed a technique akin to guerrilla warfare, as the arrival of invaders would send the men fleeing to mountain hideouts, from which they would wage ceaseless war until the enemy left. The men of Debdu were excellent horsemen, Edrehi had observed, and had trained their steeds to gallop along Debdu's twisting mountain trails at a pace that no invader could match. As for their willingness to fight to the death, Edrehi had written, "When they have war with an enemy, the enemy is sure to be conquered. . . . They would sooner kill twenty men than one Jew."

Yet what if there were no enemy to fight? How did Debdu's inhabitants then pass the time? As Slouschz talked to people and began to win their confidence, a bizarre story started to unfold. Beneath the bucolic surface, it seemed that Debdu wasn't so tranquil a place after all—enemy or no enemy. Lacking an invader to rally against, the people of Debdu would simply fight one another.

Most of the fighting appeared to involve the village's two most prominent families, splitting the community into two desperate, feuding camps. On the one side were the Cohans, the city's traditionally leading family. The clan boasted roots that traced back to fourteenth-century Seville, from which they had departed at the start of the Marrano conversions. Arrayed against them was a clan of aggressive Sephardic newcomers, the Morcianos, who hailed from Murcia in southeastern Spain, apparently arriving following the Inquisition a century later.

Considering the passions that had been aroused in the matter, the issue that divided the two families seemed unbelievably petty: which side held the stronger claim to a one-half interest in one of Debdu's seventeen synagogues.

Yet petty or not, the quarrel had apparently been going on for quite a while. How long? When he made inquiries, Slouschz couldn't believe his ears. This wasn't a fight of a year or two at all. This was a quarrel that had gone on uninterrupted—and unresolved—for a stupefying three hundred years. Year after year, decade after decade, generation after generation. Always and endlessly the question came down to this: Who owned the synagogue—the Morcianos or the Cohans?

Along the way, everyone in Debdu had taken sides. Behind the high cliffs of Debdu, half the families supported the Cohans and the other half supported the Morcianos. Thus arrayed, the two groups appeared to Slouschz to have "lived for centuries in a state of continuous social antagonism."

There had been quarreling, backbiting, fighting, and even killings. From one local resident, Slouschz learned of an incident that had occurred more than thirty years earlier but might have happened only the day before: A group of three Morcianos had left Debdu on horseback for a business trip to a neighboring village. Five days later their bodies were found riddled with bullets and slashed by knives. The murders were never solved.

When Slouschz approached the Debdu rabbinical council for some perspective on how the situation had managed to get so totally out of hand, he was shown a two-hundred-year-old rabbinical scroll by way of explanation. The document, drafted by a Cohan when the fight had already been under way for a century, portrayed the Morcianos as a nasty, contentious lot, who'd arrived from Murcia, sweet-talked their way into an influential role in the synagogue's affairs, then promptly ousted the Cohans and renamed the place as their own.

Thereafter, the Morcianos appear to have gotten lawyers to ratify their claim—not simply to the synagogue, but to the land under it as well. According to the scroll, the Morcianos then began going around saying, "We have a legal statement given to us by Rabbi Judah (may his light shine), which says that one half of the synagogue belongs to the Beni Morciano."

When the local council couldn't resolve the matter, the Morcianos took the issue up the hierarchical ladder to the Sephardic rabbinical council in Fez. When they failed to get satisfaction even there, Slouschz was told, a succeeding generation of Morcianos went all the way to the Grand Rabbinical Council in Jerusalem. But no lasting solution emerged from that effort either. Each new generation brought a new compromise, each new compromise would eventually fall apart and the fighting would begin again—leaving an ever-accumulating mountain of records and documents, in rabbinical archives from Fez to Jerusalem, to fuel yet more fighting.

It was as if the Morcianos and the Cohans had become trapped in some eternal cycle of quarreling and rancor, prisoners of a petty and meaningless little Ur-argument that had grown into a vast and enveloping dispute, bigger than even Debdu itself. When one family proclaimed itself head of the community, the other would pop up with a counter-claim. When a Cohan opened a shop in front of a Morciano neighborhood, the Morcianos immediately went to Fez, complaining of a Cohan plot. Generation after generation it went on, then lifetime after lifetime, as the two sides maneuvered and schemed to turn every issue to their advantage in the quarrel that underpinned everything: Who owned the synagogue?

By the time Slouschz arrived on the scene, the situation had gotten so oppressive that many Debdu families had simply packed up and left. Records in the archives of the Alliance Israelite Universelle in Paris reveal that in 1903, unrest in Debdu had left many Jews hungry and in some cases homeless. In his journal Slouschz toted up the numbers of families that had left in the meantime and the communities to which they had fled. Three families had gone to Casablanca; five to Tangier; eight to Algiers; and to the nearby village of Ras-el-Ain—which the French army had recently seized, occupied and renamed Berguent—a full twenty.

Thereafter, Slouschz as well departed, and returning to Paris, he drafted his manuscript and sent it to a publishing house in America. The publisher had modest success with the volume, selling something over two thousand copies to local Jewish study groups and archives, and the book soon dropped out of print.

With that, the curtain of obscurity once again descended upon the odd little mountain village of Debdu, and its suffocating world of quarreling and scheming.

Or did it?

In 1923, one of the Morciano families that had settled in Berguent gave birth to a son named Simon. And twenty years later, Simon became a rabbi in the Sephardic faith. And in obedience to the Talmudic commandment to be fruitful and multiply, he fathered four sons. And in the fullness of time the sons emigrated to Europe, and then to America. And scarcely had they set foot in their newfound land than they got into a quarrel—and the cycle of Debdu began again.

Chapter 2

On a summerlike day in 1985, a group of five men—three from Los Angeles and two from New York—arrived at the front entrance of Number One St. Andrews Plaza, a large and forbidding federal office building in New York City. Two of the visitors were private investigators, one was a lawyer, one was a businessman, and the fifth was a government civil servant. All wore suits and ties, and collectively they exuded a businesslike air as they stepped inside to have their briefcases (and themselves) searched for explosives or concealed weapons.

This was a ritual indignity that anyone entering the offices of the U.S. Attorney for the Southern District of New York was learning to endure. Authorities had lately picked up indications that a Libyan hit team was planning an attack on the building—apparently to assassinate the U.S. Attorney, Rudolph Giuliani—and security precautions were suddenly turning up everywhere.

In a way it was no surprise. Giuliani had been on the job for just over two years of a four-year term, and bombs and death threats were becoming an almost daily occurrence, as the boss on the eighth floor kept hammering home the point—in courtrooms and press conferences alike—that the Southern District stood ready to take on anyone, from Middle Eastern terrorists to the dons of organized crime.

Under Giuliani's predecessors, the Southern District had developed an esprit de corps unmatched in any other Justice Department field office. Its cases were bigger and more complex, its defendants richer and more cunning, than anywhere else.

Yet now under Giuliani, a new element of danger had been added, as if the decade-old office building had become a kind of Fort Apache in the wilderness of late-century American crime. It was something that every occupant of the building could feel—an almost electric sense of excitement and even peril in simply turning up for work in the morning.

For thirty years presidents and the public had worried over the spread of crime and violence in American life, yet here at St. Andrews Plaza it seemed as if things were at last coming to a head. A charismatic and ambitious U.S. Attorney, imbued with a sense of mission that many of his predecessors had seemed to lack, had rallied around him some of the brightest young prosecutors in the government. As was the case throughout federal law enforcement, they were underpaid and overworked, and under Giuliani the workload seemed to grow heavier by the day. No one had secretaries, Xerox machines were constantly breaking, and offices were a riot of papers, memos, and pleadings stacked on the floor and tumbling out of filing cabinets.

Yet no one seemed to mind, as the corridors of St. Andrews Plaza had begun to throb with a sense of urgency and purpose. In the Gospel of John is told the story of how Andrew the Fisherman left his nets at Capernaum to follow Christ for three years in his ministry on earth. And in the building that now bore his name a similar sense of mission had begun to spread. From the U.S. marshals on the second floor, to the top aides to Giuliani on the eighth and the Organized Crime Unit offices that people couldn't even enter without a passkey on the ninth, it was as if a great historical adventure had begun.

Though the faces of the visitors would have betrayed little sign of emotion as they placed their attaché cases on the conveyor belt and stepped one after another through the archlike metal detectors, all were uneasy at the symbolism of the moment. It was a symbolism only they could have appreciated, for though they bore no guns or explosives, the damage they ultimately hoped to cause, in a sense, could scarcely have been worse if they were to have whipped out machine pistols and started spraying bystanders with bullets.

In fact, the men were not agents of Black September, but representatives of Guess* Inc. of Beverly Hills, a fast-growing West Coast manufacturer of denim jeans fashions. They had come for a secret meeting with federal prosecutors. The men told each other that what they were doing was required by the law and inspired by civic virtue. Yet privately, they must have known that the real reason they were

* Technically, the company name includes a question mark; for readability, the device is not used in this book.

there was to serve a darker end. In the biblical spirit of the scheming brothers of Joseph, they were about to stab some former friends in the back.

Though the evidence they brought was circumstantial, they hoped it would inspire a federal criminal tax fraud case against a rival business firm in New York—Jordache Enterprises. With luck, Jordache's owners would wind up in prison. The men from Guess wanted their rivals behind bars because Jordache's owners awkwardly happened to own half the stock in Guess itself. For the last two years the Guess people had been fighting to get the stock back, and getting the Jordache people locked up as tax criminals seemed like a good way to gain some advantage in the struggle.

The reason the Guess people wanted the stock back was simple. They'd sold their shares for $4.7 million, and two years later the stock was worth many times that amount.

The folks at Jordache had bought the stock free, clear, and legally. Yet the sellers were not about to take the loss lying down. They were four brothers from Morocco, their names were Marciano, and their father was a rabbi. And every time they sought consolation in the words of Talmudic scripture, it was as if the nation of Abraham rose up as one to condemn the outrage. When a buyer underpays, it constitutes a "fraud on the Torah." If unfair advantage is taken of one of the parties to a business transaction and the other party makes a profit greater than one-sixth of the thing's value, the transaction may be nullified, and the wronged party may demand the return of the article in question—as if no sale had occurred. Exchange of coins or even money does not constitute a sale. In fact, nothing makes a sale when one side cheats the other.

The Marcianos knew very well that the law of the Torah did not apply in the state of California. Yet it certainly helped to know that God was on their side, especially considering the strategy they had undertaken to pursue. To recover their stock, the Marcianos had recently filed suit in California state court, charging that the Nakashes had fraudulently induced them to sell their shares. To bolster that claim, the Marcianos now proposed to reveal the Nakashes as criminals as well.

The leader of the group was Paul Marciano, the youngest of the four brothers. There was something in his eyes that even strangers would notice—a restless, unsettled, roving quality—and on this particular day his energy seemed at its peak, as he grabbed his briefcase from the conveyor belt once it emerged from the metal detector, and headed inside.

It was perhaps because of Paul that the men were even in New York at all, for in many ways it seemed as if Paul had been the one who had encouraged his brothers to sell their shares in the first place—or at least to part with them in a fifty-fifty split instead of selling the company outright. Now as the elevator ascended—past the Narcotics Unit on the second floor, the Civil Division on the fourth and fifth, the Securities Fraud Unit on the sixth—and lurched to a halt at the seventh floor offices of the chief of the Criminal Division, it was Paul who was leading them in the fight to get the stock back.

The events that had brought the group to the steps of St. Andrews Plaza had begun two years earlier in a suite of rooms in the Beverly Hilton Hotel. It was there that the Marciano brothers of Beverly Hills —new to America and hungry for opportunity—had sold half the stock in their promising young company, Guess, to the Nakash brothers of Brooklyn. The price had looked like big money at the time. But Guess had grown so rapidly thereafter that the sale seemed in retrospect to have been little more than a gift. As a result, Paul was willing to do almost anything, including becoming a government informant, to get the stock back—and his brothers had gone along.

Fingering one's business partners as tax criminals might have been an accepted business practice in some parts of the world, but it was hardly an everyday occurrence for most people, and behind the meeting lay weeks of debate as the men had quarreled among themselves over whether to take the fateful step.

One of the most reluctant of all had been the Marcianos' own attorney in the matter, a mustached California trial lawyer named Marshall Grossman. A civil litigator by training and experience, Grossman knew little about criminal law, and even less about how to deal with federal prosecutors in New York's Southern District. Involving them in this matter might set in motion forces that no one could control.

But whether or not it was because the Marcianos were paying him a great deal of money for his legal advice, Grossman had in the end put his doubts aside and decided to go forward. As a result, he now stood inside St. Andrews Plaza along with his client, waiting for an elevator to take them all upstairs.

At Grossman's side stood a private investigator named Bruce Dollar.

The private eye, who worked for the New York investigative firm of Kroll Associates, had done the legwork that had led to the evidence that the Guess men now wanted to use against the Nakashes.

A balding onetime member of the New York City Board of Education, who had married the sister of the owner of the firm, Dollar conveyed wariness and suspicion in his every move, from his darting eyes to a habit of answering questions by asking, "Why do you want to know?" Yet he was also a bit of a boaster, and seemed to enjoy regaling members of the press with stories of his exploits. Dollar would tell of auto chases along the cliffs of the French Riveria, of "sting" operations to recover stolen property, of using hidden microphones to catch white-collar crooks.

This was Dollar's world, and recently he had been stalking its remotest frontiers, from the Orient to Central America, from Seventh Avenue to North Africa and the Middle East, on behalf of Guess. Like the spies of the Roman plutocrat Marcus Licinius Crassus, who spent their time gathering evidence of scandal for Crassus to use against his enemies in court, Dollar had been sent forth to scour the earth in search of dirt to throw at the Nakashes when the fraud case got to trial.

"I've been to over twenty countries on this case," he once declared. "You name it, I went there."

Though the trial was still months—and maybe even years—away, it looked as if Dollar had lately come up with something too nasty and incriminating to keep under wraps. In the sweatshops of Hong Kong's Kowloon Peninsula, where Jordache jeans were manufactured, he had stumbled across what looked like a Nakash-directed tax and customs fraud scheme.

In an interview years later, Dollar acknowledged that he knew little about the garment industry, and even less about the mysteries of business in Asia—at least when the case first began. But from what he did know, and from what he could find out in public records on file in the Crown Colony, it seemed to him that the Nakashes were using certain Jordache-controlled exporting companies in Hong Kong to inflate the cost of locally manufactured Jordache garments being exported to the United States. If so, the move would have lowered Jordache taxable income in the United States while simultaneously boosting the amount of money held by Jordache abroad.

When he presented this evidence to the Marcianos in Los Angeles, no one knew quite what to do, for it seemed that at least some of the fraudulent activity involved a Guess subsidiary. Though the subsidiary was being run by the Nakashes out of their offices in New York, the operation was actually owned by Guess, which made the Marcianos at least partly responsible if the company was being used as a tax fraud.

"It's a question of fiduciary responsibility," one of the Marciano accountants, a former IRS official named Iskowitz, told them. "You'd better report this to the government or you could be in hot water. It'll look like you were involved in it." Lawyers from a Los Angeles firm that specialized in customs and importing matters confirmed the advice, so the Marcianos took action.

That was where the next man in the group came in. His name was Ronald Saranow, he was head of the Criminal Investigation Division of the IRS in Los Angeles, and he had been asked by IRS officials in New York to join the Guess people for the meeting. Saranow had become involved rather by accident. It happened because Iskowitz, the Marciano accountant, had asked for a meeting with the IRS brass in L.A. Since the meeting was apparently going to involve criminal allegations, Saranow attended in his position as head of the Criminal Division.

At the L.A. meeting, which had taken place in Paul Marciano's home, a box of photocopied documents, receipts, and some civil court depositions had been handed over. Unfortunately, since the information involved taxpayers who resided back east, the Los Angeles office had no jurisdiction, and Saranow had contacted the IRS in New York. Not long afterward, a rumpled IRS investigator named Steve Levy arrived to interview the Marcianos on the matter.

Thereafter, the L.A. office had sent Levy the materials from Marciano. Yet back in New York, the case seemed to get buried in Levy's in-basket, at least so far as the Marcianos could tell. The days turned into weeks, and the summer began to slip by. Was the IRS going to pursue the matter at all? A way had to be found to get it off the back burner.

That was where the fifth man in the group came in. His name was Bart Schwartz, and he too worked for Kroll. Short, thin, and with a fondness for houndstooth tweeds, Schwartz might well have played the part of an Oxford don. In fact, he had only recently left the Justice Department, where he had worked as head of the Criminal Division in the Southern District.

New to Kroll and eager to lend a hand in what was shaping up as a major piece of business, Schwartz had spotted an opportunity to be helpful. To get a criminal case going, the IRS usually needs a grand jury. But grand juries require a prosecutor. So to get one, Schwartz had volunteered to speak to a prosecutor he happened to know quite well indeed, his own successor as chief of the Criminal Division, Howard Wilson.

A pudgy-faced lawyer with wire-rimmed glasses and a friendless stare, Wilson until recently had run the Civil Division, where he'd made a name for himself fighting environmentalists over New York's multi-billion-dollar Westway project. Now Giuliani had moved Wilson over to the criminal side, but he was so new to the job that he was still feeling his way into the world of federal law enforcement. Eventually, Wilson would undoubtedly encounter the case anyway, but Schwartz figured it certainly couldn't hurt to give a leg up right now—especially since Wilson was increasingly being viewed around the office as Giuliani's most trusted aide and confidant.

"We'll be doing Howard a favor," Dollar later quoted Schwartz as reassuring him. "It'll be a kind of 'help you out' type arrangement."

When Schwartz at last spoke to Wilson he was reassuring. "It's a good case," he said. "Wait until you see, it's almost a blueprint for fraud in the garment district."

Now, here they all were—lawyers, private eyes, prosecutors, an IRS agent—all gathered in Wilson's corner office to discuss the case. Would Wilson get behind the matter and agree to pursue it, or would he view the allegations as too remote and confusing to bother with at all?

Everyone had taken chairs, with Wilson stepping from behind his desk to be introduced to his visitors by Schwartz. Then the discussion began, though it had not gotten very far before Schwartz swung the conversation around to the question of "immunity." All had agreed that this was a necessary precondition to cooperating in a criminal investigation. And since Schwartz had arranged the meeting, it seemed only proper that he should be the one to bring the issue up.

Immunity was necessary, Schwartz explained, because once the Nakashes got wind of the meeting they could be counted on to fight back with trumped-up charges of their own.

"We've got to have protection from that," Schwartz declared. "The Marcianos need immunity from prosecution arising from their roles as government informants. Is that something that can be arranged? You understand."

Wilson nodded, and the meeting proceeded, as the men from Los Angeles began to reel off their claim of having been innocently roped into a Nakash-directed tax and customs fraud run out of Hong Kong.

By the end of the hour, Wilson had heard enough. In one sense it was all terribly confusing and remote. But there was obviously something to it. And besides, the charges came with the personal endorsement of his own predecessor on the job, Schwartz.

The question was, where would Wilson assign the case? Organizationally, the Southern District's Criminal Division had been divided into six separate units, each reporting to Wilson, and through him, to Giuliani. Lowest rung on the ladder was General Crimes, a kind of training ground for new assistant prosecutors when they first came aboard. Normally, people would stay in the unit—known derisively around the office as "Little Crimes"—for eight to nine months, handling simple matters such as check forgeries or the routine bank frauds that result from providing bogus information on loan applications. Thereafter, the young prosecutors would be moved on to one of the more specialized units: Narcotics, Organized Crime, Securities Fraud, Public Corruption, or Major Crimes.

As Wilson sized the matter up, the Jordache investigation would clearly belong in Major Crimes, which handled many of the largest and most complex cases that didn't automatically belong with one of the other units. But who in the unit should be given the case?

Sitting at Wilson's elbow was a man named Marty Perschetz, who had just that question in mind. Perschetz had only recently been made head of the Major Crimes Unit under Wilson, and after the meeting broke up, he and his boss would obviously have some consulting to do.

One possibility for the assignment was a young assistant prosecutor named Lorna Schofield, who had joined the Southern District the previous spring after a tour as a junior associate at the law firm of Cleary, Gottlieb, Steen & Hamilton. "I had come to the Southern District to learn how to be a litigator," she said later. "I wanted to learn how cases worked, and I wanted to learn how to deal with juries. It was the kind of thing you just never got the chance to do as a junior associate at one of the firms."

Schofield was not a person one easily forgot. Her name to the contrary, she was a young woman of Filipino heritage. She was bright, hardworking, had gone to college in Indiana, and had thereafter come east to attend law school in New York.

Schofield was as ambitious and aggressive as anyone in the office. But a fluky bureaucratic assignment seemed to have stalled her career almost before it began. The case involved a "Black Liberation Army" investigation that Giuliani had wrestled away from a rival U.S. Attorney in Brooklyn. Wiretaps had been put in place, and at the appointed hour, rifle-toting FBI agents in flak jackets had swooped down on the homes of suspected revolutionary radicals from Brooklyn to Massachusetts. Charges ranged from fraud and weapons counts, to conspiracy to commit murder, arson, robbery, and racketeering.

The Major Crimes Unit prosecutor assigned to the case was a young man named Ken Ross. But paperwork had exploded as defense lawyers like the flamboyant William Kunstler had rushed in to try to politicize the proceedings. Ross soon found himself overwhelmed and began asking for help. One thing had led to another, and before long Schofield was sent over from General Crimes to help out.

At the trial, Schofield had done her best. But the evidence in the case turned out to be flimsy, and after five days of deliberations, the jury acquitted everyone of all but a few minor infractions. Now, more than a month later, Schofield was still languishing in Major Crimes—a free body, looking for something to do. Perhaps, thought Perschetz, here was a job to give her. And even if the case proved too complex and technical for a novice to handle, what did it matter? After all, tax cases in the Southern District pretty much tended to be handled by the boys over at IRS anyway.

This was interesting, Wilson agreed at last, perhaps shifting his ample frame to signal the approaching end to the meeting. And yes, he went on, he would certainly look into the matter of immunity.

As the group stepped into the sunlight, Paul Marciano turned to look for Saranow, apparently to ask for the IRS man's views on how the meeting had gone, but the official was no longer to be seen. Like ice on the sidewalk he had simply melted away, apparently—as one of the group later explained—to check in with a friend elsewhere in the building.

Paul turned to his lawyer, Grossman, and volunteered a thought. "He is tough," he said, speaking of Wilson, "tough! But he is going to be fair. It was an excellent meeting."

Grossman wasn't so sure. As he had read Wilson, the man had come across as skeptical of the whole story—as if he seemed to find it less than credible that a tax fraud of such apparent scope could be unfolding without the Marcianos' actually knowing and even participating in it.

"It was like a police lineup," Grossman recalled later. "Very unnerving."

Yet it was too late to worry about that now, and to all appearances Paul hardly seemed to care anyway. Let Grossman fret all he wanted about what Wilson might have thought. Paul's own fears might have been drowned instead by the rush of beating wings. The Greeks may have had their serpent-headed Furies, but Jews had demons too. And as the men from Guess stepped out the door of St. Andrews Plaza and into the summer sun, Ashmodai, Lilith, and Dumai went with them, to punish with their secret stings the crimes of all who escape public justice.

Chapter 3

A twenty-minute cab ride up Sixth Avenue sat the offices of Jordache Enterprises. Precisely what Avi Nakash, at thirty-nine the youngest of the three Nakash brothers, might have been doing in them on this fateful day is a detail lost in the obscurity of the quarrel's beginnings. He might have been meeting with customers in the cramped and cluttered storage room that doubled as Jordache's on-premises conference center. Or he might have told his secretary to send out for lunch, and eaten at his desk, something he often did.

Yet whatever he was doing, one thing is certain: Thoughts of the Marcianos were not far from his mind. Though he had no idea of the forces being gathered against him by the brothers downtown, Avi no longer trusted his business partners in Beverly Hills any more than they trusted him.

It was the lawsuit that the Marcianos had filed to get back their stock that had Avi upset.

From virtually the moment he had laid eyes on their lawsuit complaint, Avi had realized he was dealing with dangerous people. The lies, the distortions! What kind of business partners would make up things like that?

Avi knew, of course, that there is always at least a kernel of truth in the words of the slanderer. Yet as their name suggested, the Nakashes *

---

* Nakash appears originally to have been an Islamic name, and is still encountered in the Arab world as well as in Iran. It is derived from the Arabic word "nakashsha," meaning etcher of metal. In Hebrew, Nakash is not commonly encountered as a surname. The nearest noun—"Nachash" or "Nahash"—refers to a snake or serpent demon. In the Torah, the word appears as both a proper noun and title, and refers to the King of the Ammonites, a vassal tribe of cruel idolaters who were constantly at war with the Hebrew people.

were not ones to slander too freely. In Leviticus (19:16) it is written, "Thou shalt not go up and down as a talebearer among thy people." In fact, according to certain sages in the Gemara, the spreading of yarns can be as evil a pursuit as murder or adultery. But considering the circumstances, no cautionary finger wagging from the Torah was going to stop Avi Nakash. He and his brothers were ready to fight back.

In fact, with the help of their lawyers, the brothers from Brooklyn had been hard at work for months on a counterattack. To others, the accumulating documents might have looked like little more than smears and libels. Yet to Avi and his brothers, the evidence was overwhelming: Out in L.A. the Marcianos were robbing them blind.

As far as Avi was concerned, the Marcianos were nothing more than fraudsters and thieves. How had he ever let himself get tangled up with these people? It was a question he and his brothers had no doubt asked themselves a lot lately, and the answer no doubt was always the same —they'd been the biggest asses in the history of the jeans game.

Like the Marcianos, the Nakashes were Jewish immigrants. One side of their family traced to the Jewish community of Baghdad, Iraq, and the other to a once-thriving community of Sephardic* Jews in Aleppo in eastern Syria.

By the early twentieth century, the politics of prejudice and persecution had decimated these communities of Syrian and Iraqi Jews, and among those who fled were the Nakashes, coming to rest eventually in Tel Aviv, where Josef, the oldest of three sons, was born in 1943.

In Israel, the Nakashes had been a poor family, so poor in fact that the second of the three brothers, Ralph, had been sent to a kibbutz to cut down on the number of mouths to feed after the third youngster, Abraham (Avi, for short), was born. Ralph himself had never gotten beyond the eighth grade before going to work, and eventually into the army.

As the oldest of the three, Joe was the first to emigrate, arriving in the United States in 1962 at the age of twenty-one. With twenty-five dollars in his pocket and speaking no English, he wound up sleeping on park benches and in subway stations, while he scoured the garment shops of the city's Lower East Side, looking for a job.

It was an inauspicious beginning for a young man with big dreams.

* Many people tend to misuse the word "Sephardic" to describe all Arab-world Jews, when it actually refers only to Jews who emigrated from Spain during the fourteenth and fifteenth centuries.

Here he was, Joe Nakash, a penniless nobody, alone on the streets of New York—scarcely more than a teenager as America's worship of youth erupted all around him. Poverty might have been no disgrace, it was true—but it was certainly no great honor, either.

One well-trodden path for immigrant Jews from Israel had been to become salesmen in discount electronics shops, setting the price of an item by gauging how much might be squeezed from the customer. Another route might have been to go to work for one of the garment manufacturers in the silk underwear business—a trade in which Syrian Jews had a virtual monopoly.

No such opportunities developed, and eventually Joe found a job as a stock clerk for a Brooklyn discount store. He saved his money, and in 1966 invited his brothers to come and join him. In time they opened a discount store selling cut-rate jeans from makers like Lee's and Levi Strauss, and by the mid-1970s had built it into a four-store chain.

Then in 1977, in the middle of a night of vandalism brought on by a citywide power blackout, the largest Nakash store was torched and looted. The insurance underwriter paid off $120,000 on the policy, presenting the brothers with an opportunity they'd been hoping to seize for some time: to get into the business of manufacturing jeans for themselves.

The time seemed right for such a move. Sales of basic "five-pocket" denim trousers—long the mainstay of companies such as Levi Strauss —had begun to fade as youthful, status-conscious shoppers switched more and more to better-fitting trousers from women's fashion designers such as Gloria Vanderbilt and Calvin Klein.

Clearly, the market was there. But how could three Jewish brothers from Brooklyn tap into it? The prospects looked bleak when Ralph brought back some samples stitched together by a sweatshop in Hong Kong and tried to drum up orders at a trade fair in the Statler Hilton.

"No one believed we were going to make it," Joe later told an interviewer.

To get into the game, the brothers needed a gimmick, something new and unique. After all, they agreed, you can't chew with somebody else's teeth.

Steeped in the Middle Eastern arts of obliqueness and guile, the brothers seemed manipulative by nature. And as the youngest of the three, Avi's guile certainly showed through when he came up with the gimmick that would make them all rich. Catching on quickly to the American way of doing things, he suggested that they forget about the product and invest in the image instead. In other words, spend the money on an ad campaign.

For "Nakash" jeans to be a hit, the brothers likewise needed a better, more European-sounding name than they had. But this proved no problem, for in the spirit of their newfound land, they simply made one up—Jordache. And since the jeans were to be manufactured in a sweatshop in Hong Kong, and since 1977 was the Year of the Horse in the Chinese calendar, the brothers came up with the head of a horse, its mane flying rakishly, as the label's logo.

But what should be the theme of the ad campaign? To Joe, the answer was obvious. This was America, wasn't it? And what more mesmerized the masses than sex, wealth, and social power, the ultimate totems of arriviste achievement in the late 1970s? If a four-dollar swatch of denim could be turned into such a symbol of success, there was just no telling how much people would be willing to pay for it.

So Joe wrote a commercial, and with a loan from a bank the brothers produced it. The spot featured a tousle-haired blonde wearing some skin-tight "Jordache" denims (and apparently topless) astride a horse galloping through the surf. Suddenly a lithe young olive-skinned man with a generally Mediterranean look about him leaped into the scene and vaulted onto the horse. As the two galloped off through foam and mist, a jingle repeated: "Jordache has the look that's right. . . . You got the look I want to know better."

It wasn't exactly a Kama Sutran love chant, but to teenage girls looking to fill an emptiness and longing in one of the more trying stages of life, it might as well have been. Not since Tabu perfume scandalized an earlier generation with a *New Yorker* advertisement featuring a woman swept back in the embrace of a violinist overcome by the scent of her cologne had people encountered a mass market ad more blatantly directed at sexual fantasy. This ad didn't just arouse expectation and desire; this ad promised instant escape into a world like nothing in real life—galloping stallions, pounding surf, and half-naked young men who leaped from nowhere to seize topless teenagers in their thrusting embrace.

The three networks all rejected the spot as lewd, but New York area independents agreed to carry it, and within weeks Jordache was the rage of every high school in the Greater New York area, even as bedazzled Madison Avenue executives scrambled to figure out who these mysterious geniuses were. Two months earlier, this company was not even known to exist. Yet now, for all anyone knew, Jordache might as well have been *The House of Jordache S.A.,* complete with an upstairs salon on the Rue St. Honoré for the last seventy years. Like a garment industry version of Häagen-Dazs ice cream, another New York–based consumer product that had sprung from nowhere with a chic-sounding foreign name, Jordache had acquired instant credibility and status as a "quality import" by the singular expedient of an invented moniker and some blatantly suggestive advertising.

Within months, Joe was explaining the secret of his success to *Time* magazine this way: "Psychologically, it looked like there was a big company behind Jordache. The strategy worked." Not long after that and he was confessing the real secret to *People* magazine, saying, "When a woman or a man wears Jordache jeans, I want them to feel sexier, which is not so bad." A model in one of the commercials got right to the point, telling the reporter, "Jordache likes the ass shot."

Within a year, the Nakash brothers had sold $75 million worth of their jeans and were awash in money. They branched into banking, and soon were the second-largest shareholders in one of the fastest-growing banks in Israel. They bought summer homes in Deal, a resort town on the Jersey shore that had become popular with prosperous Syrian Jews. They moved into shipping and bought a fleet of freighters. They named the company Yama Shipping, created an ensign emblazoned with the Jordache horse emblem, and put the fleet's management in the hands of a Brooklyn real estate broker whom Avi had met one day while walking along the beach. They expanded their production in Hong Kong and began setting up Jordache International retail outlets throughout Asia.

And every time the brothers stopped to think about what had happened to them, their rags-to-riches saga must have seemed too good to be true. From literally nothing at all, they had become the high priests of the designer jeans industry—the *Cohanim* of denim fashion. In biblical history, the nation of the Canaanites is sometimes referred to as the "land of the purple" for its trade in fabric dyes. But not even the conquests of Joshua brought greater bounty to the victors than what Avi and his brothers had reaped on Fashion Avenue. They'd wandered out of the desert and straight into starring roles in an eighties era remake of *I Can Get It for You Wholesale.* As Joe told a magazine writer in a comment that was quoted everywhere, "I'm no longer interested in making money. Money can always be earned. Now I'm show business."

It was the alchemy of consumer advertising that had made all this possible. Advertising had been the key to the riches of Pharaoh that Joe had been seeking since he had first arrived in the promised land two decades earlier. Where else but America were such things possible? No longer was he Joe Nakash, *schmatte* merchant. Now he was Clark Gable in *The Hucksters,* fast-talking Sidney Greenstreet while he waltzed around Ava Gardner in a deal-a-minute world of glitz and dreams. There were limousines to take the Nakashes everywhere, public relations consultants to turn out Broadway celebrities for parties in their honor at places like New York's Tavern on the Green. It was too amazing for words; half of forty years in the desert, and now this.

And what better moment than the dawn of the 1980s, with its fixation on instant wealth and gratification for every two-income sub-urban homesteader in posthistorical America? Here they were, the brothers Nakash, uneducated immigrants in a business of pushcarts and peddlers, and by the fortune of the gods they'd hit upon the biggest markup of all time—designer jeans. Now they were no longer Seventh Avenue garmentoes but Heroes of Capitalism, as such publi-cations as *The New York Times* and *Business Week* ran ponderous stories on their management strategies and plans for the future.

Could this go on forever? From three of the poorest urchins in Israel could Joe, Ralph and Avi Nakash become the three richest men on Fashion Avenue? By the summer of 1982 there was reason to worry that their luck might soon run out, as recession started to pinch con-sumer spending. Among those that looked vulnerable was Jordache, which had begun pursuing an aggressive licensing strategy that would eventually wind up putting its name on everything from windbreakers to school tote bags. By thus moving "down market," the company seemed in peril of the sort of sales slump that often hits first at the low end of the retail clothing business.

That was when an Israeli deal promoter named Hardof Wolf turned up, wandering into the situation like Ezekiel into the Valley of the Bones. With him he brought news of an investment opportunity in a small but thriving California jeans company—Guess Inc. of Beverly Hills.

Guess had a hot product, Wolf explained—a pipe-stem-thin denim trouser, with zippered cuffs and a fabric with a supple, worn feel that the company achieved by putting bolts of the material through indus-trial wash cycles with actual pumice stones thrown into the machines.

The technique was destroying washing machines throughout Los Angeles, but it was also producing garments that were rapidly becoming the rage of Southern California.

When Wolf told the Nakashes how much these jeans were selling for, the brothers' eyes must have bugged out. Jordache "Basics" went for thirty-five dollars and under at retail, but these Guess jeans were going for up to twice as much—and the company couldn't keep up with the demand. They needed money to expand, and without it they might lose the very market niche they'd found.

Joe and Ralph weren't much interested, but Avi seems to have spotted a big opportunity—especially for himself personally. As the youngest of the three brothers, he had been stuck from the start with what was obviously the dreariest end of the whole operation—managing distribution—while Ralph got to strut around as Jordache's designer and Joe, as the head man and founder, got to give all the interviews and speak on television.

Now, here was a chance for Avi himself to step into the sunlight. In return for a mere $4.7 million and a promise to provide marketing and manufacturing know-how, Jordache could get half the company's stock as well as three of the six seats on its board of directors. Who could resist?

Eventually, the Marcianos came to New York for a get-acquainted meeting in Joe's house in Queens. It was a Saturday afternoon in the spring of 1983. Joe and Avi and their wives were there, and Ralph, who lived next door, saw the group gather and strolled over as well. Joe took one look at them and realized just how inexperienced they really were.

"They don't know about big business," he said after they left. "They're not in sophistication to do a big business."

That was then. Two years later, in 1985, it was Avi and his brothers who seemed to be in need of sophistication. Though he held the title of Guess's chairman of the board, it was as if Avi were powerless to deal with the very situation he had created. When the Nakashes bought their stake, the Marcianos had behaved as if $4.7 million was gold beyond counting. For treasure in such abundance they were willing not only to part with half their company, but also to sign back on as salaried employees. The Marcianos would handle the day-to-day running of things locally on the West Coast, while the worldly-wise Nakashes would take care of the global big picture from New York.

But Avi was no fool. And he knew that whatever the Marcianos might now claim to the contrary, $4.7 million was hardly enough to support the lives of Babylonian splendor the brothers had instantly acquired. Though Avi would hardly have wanted to say so, it was as if he had asked to marry the village virgin, only to have the entire synagogue keel over laughing at the wedding when the woman of his dreams turned out to be the town slut.

Or maybe it was like the story of the king and the slave.

"Go to market and buy me a fish," commanded the king.

The slave went and bought a fish, but the fish stank.

"I swear by your life," cried the king. "I will not forgive you for your stupidity, unless you accept one of three punishments. Either you eat the fish yourself, or you pay me back what it cost, or you let me give you one hundred lashes!"

"I will eat the fish," said the slave. But no sooner had he begun to eat than he felt nauseated.

"Better give me the hundred lashes," he begged the king.

So they began to count out the lashes one by one. When they had counted fifty the slave felt he was near death.

"Better let me pay for the fish!" he cried.

It was the same with Jordache. They'd eaten a rotten fish, gotten fifty lashes, and now they were paying for it too.

The one who seemed to taunt them the most was Georges. In 1982, Georges had apparently managed to get a girl in one of the Marciano boutiques pregnant and he'd married her. Yet no sooner was the ink dry on the Guess deal with Jordache than Georges and the missus and their year-old son were moving up in the world—way up, *and on Nakash money*.

To begin with, there was the house. Within weeks of getting his money, Georges walked into a real estate office and paid $1.9 million for an eleven-room, ivory-colored estate on a half-acre of land on Beverly Hills' elegant Roxbury Drive. The home was approached with a sweeping, circular drive, and before long the drive was choked with more than half a dozen cars and limousines, all a year old or newer: two Rolls-Royces, two stretch limos, a Cadillac Seville, a Lincoln Continental, and a Porsche Cabriolet. Where were they getting the money? That was what the Nakashes wanted to know.

But it wasn't just Georges. Soon his brother Paul had moved in down the street on Roxbury, in an equally elegant Tudor-style spread.

Eventually, the third brother, Maurice, bought a home on neighboring Oakhurst that seemed almost a mirror image of Georges's, while the fourth brother, Armand, by and by moved into the neighborhood too. It was as if Beverly Hills was becoming the Royal Court of Gomorrah, with the whole place filling up with Marcianos.

If Avi felt like a fool, it was small wonder. Here he was, the president of one of the biggest privately owned jeans companies in the world, doing business out of a cramped and noisy office that smelled of lox and onions. Meanwhile, piling up at his fingertips was evidence that out in L.A. the Marcianos were spending Guess money—half of which belonged to the Nakashes—to send out every day for catered pasta-and-salad luncheons from Rex, one of the most expensive restaurants on earth.

Worse still, it seemed that Georges had given a Guess corporate credit card to the wife, who had apparently been working her way down Rodeo Drive, buying everything in sight. She had been spending seven hundred dollars a month on lunches alone! Her travel expenses were averaging three thousand dollars monthly, with jaunts to England and Hawaii, and always first class. Besides which came the gardener and the maid, both paid in cash and apparently charged to the company.

Then came the most astounding revelation of all. A Chinese sewing contractor had turned up claiming that Georges was demanding kick-backs from him in return for work from Guess.

"Georges Marciano told me and my partner, Ki Bong Kim, to meet in his office," the contractor said. "He said he give us all the work we can handle if we overbill Guess and repay that amount to him at a different company." The contractor had even produced a check, signed by him, for $649 to prove it.

By now Avi had stacks of such evidence: affidavits and depositions, canceled checks and bank deposit slips. It was all there in lurid detail—the paper trail of their crimes—an octopuslike web of bank accounts for bogus companies, all of it assembled to skim the profits out of Guess before the Nakashes saw a dime of it.

To Avi, the people were thieves all right—and Avi knew how to deal with thieves.

"We decided to sue them," he explained years later. "It was *they* who were the criminals, not us!"

As far as Avi was concerned, the Marcianos' own charges were ridic-ulous. Okay, so maybe there had been a few irregularities out there in

Hong Kong; maybe a few Guess pants had somehow gotten Jordache labels stitched on them by mistake; maybe some of the goods had even gotten shipped into the United States as "samples" when they really weren't. But those were all innocent mistakes (if they'd even happened at all!), yet here were the Marcianos trying to trump them up into capital offenses.

Worst of all, now that the Marcianos had been confronted with the evidence of their own crimes—*real* crimes—they were claiming that their entire thieving arrangement not only was legal but had been approved in advance by none other than the Nakashes. They were claiming the arrangement had been set up because the Marcianos had asked the Nakashes for a raise but were constantly getting the runaround. So apparently they'd decided to just go ahead and help themselves by what they were now calling an innocent "bonus" arrangement.

The gall of these people was enough to leave Avi speechless. Take Georges and the missus, for instance. Within eighteen months the marriage had broken up. Now, she was suing for divorce, and in October 1984 the woman signed a declaration to bolster a claim for spousal and child support of thirty-five thousand dollars per month—reflecting the lifestyle she'd apparently grown accustomed to as a result of her "charge-it" jaunts along Rodeo Drive. Nakash lawyers had gotten their hands on the document, and one of its assertions was a stunner:

> Since our marriage substantial sums of cash have been delivered by one of respondent's brothers or brought home by respondent. On more than one occasion respondent has insisted that I personally count the funds. Approximately one month ago was the last occasion, and at that time I personally counted $25,000 in cash. After delivery of the cash, respondent then distributes the monies. I do not know who gets what, nor do I know the source of the funds. Other than being present on occasion when bags are received and placed in the safe, I have no independent knowledge of what goes on.

Where the money was coming from might have been a mystery to Mrs. Marciano, but it wasn't to Avi Nakash. So far as he was concerned, it was coming from the kickbacks. The Marcianos had apparently worked out deals with all sorts of different local subcontractors to charge Guess fifty cents to one dollar per garment over the agreed-upon contract price—then the subcontractor would kick back the money in cash directly to the Marcianos. Maybe millions had been skimmed in this way already.

Avi wasn't born yesterday. And he would have been the first to admit that people in the garment district had a habit of engaging in what accountants liked to call "sharp practices." But *this*? The Marcianos weren't just squeezing the occasional Korean stitching shop for a few shekels here and there; as Avi had by now uncovered, Georges had apparently set up his own subsidiaries to do the looting. But why should he be surprised? After all, the Nakashes were in New York, and Guess was out there in L.A., three thousand miles away, in the hands of Ali Baba and his *bulyok* brothers!

The evidence was overpowering. Take for example the recent deposition of a Guess production manager named Cary Nadler. Avi's lawyers had put the man under oath and started grilling him about the kickback scheme. Perhaps Nadler was the bagman for the whole racket. In his deposition he had virtually admitted as much, saying that one of his Guess duties had been to collect envelopes from Korean subcontractors for Georges or Maurice. The envelopes, he kept insisting, were for some Moroccan named Abel Eljam. In the deposition, Nadler had tried to plead that he was under a lot of emotional stress and that he didn't want to testify. Small wonder.

Meanwhile, in the wake of Nadler's deposition Maurice had suddenly vanished, and was said to be off in Israel or Europe someplace, sulking. There were rumors that his departure had followed a huge fight between himself and Georges. Could the events all be interconnected?

Among the papers in Avi's counterattack dossier was a letter from Georges. What Avi and his brothers felt about it can well be guessed, since years later they would still point to it as evidence of the most outrageous, backstabbing maneuver imaginable. The letter was apparently designed to put them on notice that the Marcianos had gone to the Treasury Department and Customs and stirred up an investigation into the way the Nakashes were running their business in Hong Kong. Clearly, it was all part of the Marciano campaign to get back their stock in Guess—a campaign that Avi wasn't going to buckle under to no matter what.

In response, Avi had shot back a letter defying the Marcianos to go ahead and do their worst. Yet this letter had simply brought a new insult from Georges.

"Be patient," Georges had written menacingly. "Just a few more days. . . . Maybe then you will realize who is going to lose. Have a good weekend."

Some situation Avi had gotten himself into! Though he might not have wanted to admit it in so many words, the facts seemed undeniable: Thanks to him, the Nakashes had invested in the High Court of Sodom —and down from the bench now stared the four judges: Liar, Falsifier, Bribe-taker, and Swindler.

Chapter 4

On a summer afternoon in 1985, a month or so after the meeting in Wilson's office, a helicopter dropped from the sky, and Paul Marciano stepped onto a desolate butte that overlooked a riverbed outside the town of Red Rock, Arizona. A British film crew had been there for two days. They were shooting a commercial—the first for the young company—and Paul had come to check on their progress.

The film's director, a young Londoner named Roger Lunn, had worked out the shot-by-shot storyboard for the commercial, but the idea for the commercial's basic message had been Paul's, and he had much riding on the outcome. If the commercial clicked with viewers, the Marcianos could be rich. If not, his brothers could—and probably would—be blaming Paul for wasting millions.

Paul might not have wanted to admit it, but in retrospect the commercial seems to have amounted almost to a power play—a move to cement his role as the brother who was really running Guess as the fight with the Nakashes worsened. Georges had never really wanted to get involved with the Nakashes—at least not in the way that had resulted—and in the beginning the fight had been handled mainly by Maurice. But now Maurice was abroad somewhere—Israel perhaps—and no one knew how to get in touch with him. Since Armand seemed determined to stay completely out of everything, it had fallen to Paul to take control.

In a way, it seemed only fair, since Paul would also have had to admit that if it hadn't been for him the Marcianos would probably never have gotten involved with the Nakashes in the first place. His older brothers had been against the deal. But just as Avi had pushed from the Nakash side, so too had Paul urged on his brothers from the Marciano side.

It was the sheer intensity of his personality that won arguments for Paul—an intensity developed from a lifetime of on-the-job training. Avi only had to contend with two older brothers to make himself heard; Paul had grown up having to drown out *three*. Now he was emerging as the most intense and domineering of all seven.

As with the Nakashes, the story of the Marcianos was one of poverty and persecution. Their roots traced back to the medieval city of Murcia in the south of Spain, and the forced conversions of the Marrano Jews to Christianity, which swept Spain in the fourteenth century. In the period that followed, pogroms spread across all of Spain, culminating in the expulsion of the Jews in the summer of 1492. In the upheaval, great numbers of Jews fled the country—the wealthiest and most educated to Portugal, the Netherlands, and the Holy Land. But the poor and the downtrodden went to North Africa instead. The Marcianos* were among the latter group, which settled eventually in the rugged Atlas Mountains of eastern Morocco, around the village of Debdu.

Though some scholars have lately argued that Jews lived a happy, oppression-free existence in Morocco thereafter, the historical record reveals regular and not infrequent eruptions of discrimination and abuse from one end of the country to the other. Wherever they settled, Jews were eventually herded into ghettolike *mellahs,* which soon became the focus of rioting and looting whenever mobs took to the streets.

Simply to survive, the Jews of Morocco began to adopt the language of their Arab overlords. As in Syria and the Near East, Judeo-Spanish gave way to Judeo-Arabic—and in the forbidding Atlas Mountains, where the Murcianos settled, Arabic exclusively. The Jews took on the customs and folkways of their Muslim neighbors as well. The record is replete with references to cultish superstitions such as the evil eye within Judeo-Arabic communities.

Clannishness had always been intense among the Arabs and Berbers, and beyond the immediate family, loyalty to abstract concepts such as the nation was virtually nonexistent. In 1908, a correspondent from *The Times* of London sailed to Morocco to cover an uprising in the south. In a dispatch to the foreign desk he reported, "The opposing

---

* According to Rabbi Shimon Murciano of Englewood, New Jersey, whose parents came from Debdu, the original spelling of the name for the entire clan was Murciano, derived from the city from which it hailed. But successive translations into French and English have produced two common alternatives—Morciano and Marciano. Rabbi Murciano's point regarding alternative spellings is borne out in research documents.

armies were largely made up of deserters from the other side." Such shifting loyalties and scheming became a feature of life among Morocco's Jews as well, as documents in the archives of the Alliance Israelite Universelle in Paris tell of well-entrenched backbiting and fighting not only between Jews and Arabs but among Jews of different socioeconomic classes.

A classmate of Paul's father in Morocco remembered him fifty years later as a nice enough man. But, he said, "The Marcianos just weren't very high-class people. What can I say? They were a bit ordinary, if that's the right word."

In fact, Jews from other parts of the world tended to view *all* Jews from Morocco in such a light. In 1949, as immigration to Israel from North Africa accelerated, an Israeli journalist published a long article in *Haaretz,* the Tel Aviv daily newspaper, concerning the Jews of Morocco. He wrote, "Here is a people whose primitiveness reaches the highest peak. Their education level borders on absolute ignorance. Still more serious is their inability to absorb anything intellectual. . . . All of them lack any skill and are, of course, penniless."

Gila Snow-Rowe, who taught Moroccan immigrants on a Negev kibbutz in the 1950s, remembered them thirty-five years later as being "very primitive" indeed. "They would wash their clothes in the toilet, then go outside to relieve themselves," she said. "We had real problems with these people."

It wasn't long after Moroccans began pouring into Israel that postwar turmoil swept the Marcianos out of Africa as well. Yet instead of following the bulk of their countrymen eastward, the family went north to Europe, coming to rest in a cramped stone cottage on Bretueuil Street, in the shadow of the Great Synagogue of Marseilles, France— with all four boys sleeping in the same crowded cot in the kitchen.

As young men, Paul and his brothers had done what Jewish émigrés to the South of France had done for generations before them; they went into the garment business. Dropping out of school at the age of fifteen,* Paul became a clerk in a local clothing store. By 1970, at the age of eighteen, he found himself a traveling necktie salesman, spicing up his evenings as a disk jockey at a local Marseilles radio station.

Armand as well had dropped out of school—also at the age of fifteen

---

* In trial testimony in 1989 Paul claimed to have done so as a result of having suffered "a major motorcycle accident."

—and he too had trouble getting started in a career, detouring first into a trade school where he studied for a time to be an ironworker.

Georges had grander dreams, yet for a time at least it was hard to tell whether he'd ever amount to much either. Like the others, he dropped out of school at the age of fifteen and hit the streets of Marseilles in search of a job. He tried being an electrician, but failed. He tried making floor tiles, but failed. He tried selling books door-to-door, and failed. For a time he tried being a bartender, but gave that up as well.

Yet there was something in his blood that he didn't really know existed, what North African Jews like to call "a feel for the cloth." For nearly five centuries, Sephardic Jews from North Africa and the south of France had dealt in a cotton fabric woven in the medieval French fortress city of Nîmes, and by and by Georges found himself being drawn to the trade. In the United States, this "textile de Nîmes," which had long since been shortened in English into "denim," was the uniform of working men and college students. But by the start of the 1970s, denim was emerging as a garment of fashion and seduction along the Cannes croisette, as young women from Rome and Munich strolled before the yachts swinging at anchor, dressed in skin-tight jeans and open-fronted denim vests that barely covered their bronzed and oiled breasts.

Georges must have been in heaven. Paul later recalled him telling his brother Maurice that he would open a boutique and design clothes for such women.

Georges was no designer. He knew little of how to sketch or how to shape fabric to form. What he knew was the feeling he apparently got when he looked at the women sipping Campari and soda under the parasols of St. Tropez and Cannes. They must have seemed so alluring yet so remote, so beguilingly different from the Algerian street sluts of Marseilles.

Together with Maurice and Armand, he formed a company— MG&A—and opened a boutique. Paul appears to have been the tag-along, perhaps being simply tolerated more than anything else. Occasionally, he would get the four of them in trouble, as when he decided to manufacture a line of T-shirts featuring pictures of the Snoopy cartoon character. Sued for copyright infringement, he wound up having to pay $2,600 in damages to United Features Syndicate and Charles Schulz, the distributor and creator of the character.

In the beginning it seems that at least some of Georges's designs followed the patterns of garments already in the market—"knock-offs" in trade jargon. But perhaps the cuts were a little tighter, the legs and waists a little snugger. In time, Paul claims, his brother became known along the Côte d'Azur as an up-and-coming young designer, and the number of boutiques multiplied to more than a dozen.

As the outlets multiplied, Maurice developed a knowledge of accounting, and apparently fancying himself something of a financier, he began urging that the brothers open a store in the United States. It would be a way to capitalize on Georges's name in France; perhaps it was also a way for Maurice to step out a bit from the lengthening shadow of his brother.

In any case, in 1977—at just around the time the Nakashes were getting into the designer jeans business in New York—the Marcianos opened a boutique in Los Angeles. The future looked bright. For one thing, designer jeans had become a sensation in the United States, and if Georges's own designs didn't prove a hit, well, the store could always sell those of others. Then in 1980 the Socialists came to power in France, and overnight the MG&A outlets ran into tax problems as the Mitterrand government passed stiff new levies on retailing operations such as theirs. The brothers put the business up for sale and left for Los Angeles. Not long afterward, Arab terrorists unleashed a wave of fire-bombings against the Marseilles Jewish community, and the home of a Marciano relative was burned to the ground. It was as if to say, Your life here is over, now look to America.

Once settled, the brothers began by finding new local manufacturers in the small but growing Los Angeles garment business and started peddling Georges's jeans to local department stores door-to-door. Young people found the style appealing, and the brand began to catch hold. But the company needed money to expand.

That was when Hardof Wolf turned up, curious to hear their story and eager to find investors. Not long afterward he was introducing them to the three Nakash brothers of Brooklyn, New York. They were also in the jeans business, Hardof explained, and as fortune would have it, they had all the money a man could ever dream of. What's more, they were looking to invest in exactly the sort of company the Marcianos had started.

Georges was apparently ambivalent about selling half the company. True, $4.7 million was a lot of money, but the Guess label was beginning to become a hit, and what if sales really took off? Then the Nakashes would get half the profits—for none of the work.

"Suppose they steal our styles," Georges worried to Paul one day, aware perhaps of how others said he himself had gotten started in the business. "What would happen then?"

Nonetheless, they'd done the deal anyway, and just as Georges had feared, no sooner had they parted with the stock than sales of Guess jeans exploded.

Even years later, Paul remembered The Signing as if it had been yesterday. Better to think of the July 1983 event as a Seventh Avenue version of *The Shining* instead, with Jack Nicholson as an axe-wielding Avi, smashing his way through Guess's defenses grinning, "Paul, I'm heere . . . !" With the passage of time the hideous event hadn't faded from his memory at all, but grown instead in vividness and intensity until it eventually loomed before him like the ultimate demonic deal: a handshake with three Beelzebubs at once.

Since lawyers and intermediaries had handled the negotiations, the signing was the first time since the gathering in Joe Nakash's house in New York months earlier that the two groups of brothers had actually met face to face. It was the summer of 1983, and this summit of sorts had been set to take place in a suite of rooms in the Beverly Hilton Hotel. Yet no sooner did they all meet and shake hands than an uncomfortable silence enveloped the room. Here they were, at the altar of business bliss, and in this garment industry version of an arranged marriage the room had fallen speechless, as if it had suddenly dawned on all concerned that after the festivities would come the consummation—and no one had bothered to get straight who would be the bride and who would be the groom.

Eventually one of the brothers suggested asking room service to send up some drinks. Back in Morocco, water would have been just the ticket—a little something to "sweeten the judgment" (as the locals would put it) for the feast to follow. Back in Morocco, one of the women might even have turned up with a tray of cakes and radishes to help put everybody really at ease. Back in Morocco they'd call it making a *berakha*. Back in Morocco . . .

But this wasn't back in Morocco. It was around the corner from Rodeo Drive in Beverly Hills, California, and the room wasn't full of other Moroccans, it was full of lawyers and Syrians.

Orders were taken, and like a brief summer breeze that ripples a lake before the arrival of a thunderhead, the faintest hint of a disagreement broke out. It seems the Marcianos, who hadn't yet even gotten their hands on the Nakash money—yet according to the Nakashes were already talking about buying fancy spreads for themselves in Beverly Hills—wanted to send out for Perrier. By contrast, the Nakashes of New York—who were already on their way to becoming demibillionaires—thought Perrier was a bit much. As far as they were concerned, seltzer would do just fine.

It had been straight downhill from there. "They don't look you in the eye," Paul would tell friends. "They mumble and put their hands over their mouths so you can't hear what they're saying."

Within five months of the signing, the Marcianos had filed suit in federal court in California, charging fraud and breach of contract, as well as adding an allegation of a type that was then emerging as a trendy new count in civil litigation—that the Nakashes were racketeers under the Racketeer Influenced Corrupt Organizations Act (RICO). The effort seemed weak on proof and didn't get very far, and two months later the judge dismissed the case. But Paul would have none of it, and promptly started lobbying to try all over again. In November of 1984, the charges were refiled in state court in modified form, and when Paul thereafter gave the case to Grossman, things began to improve.

Since then, Paul had been working himself to a higher and higher pitch of outrage. After all, weren't these Nakash people thieves, and didn't everyone say so?

No one had to fill Paul in on the rumors—baseless though they may have been—because he'd heard them all: The Nakashes employed gangsters and thieves; they dealt with crooked banks. They were an Israeli version of the Cosa Nostra, with tentacles that reached everywhere.

Now, with so much water under the bridge already, Paul had come to Arizona to make his commercial—a commercial that, if it succeeded, would (ironically enough) put money in the pockets of the hated Nakash. Paul had hired Roger Lunn to help him with the commercial on a recommendation from Maurice, who had known the man from back in the old days in France. But as Lunn later recalled of the time, perhaps the real reason Paul had hired him was because Lunn's operation was small and inexpensive. Moreover, since it was based in Britain and had never done business in the United States, it had no ties to any American ad agency, which meant that Paul could hire it directly, saving himself a 15 percent commission.

On the other hand, there was something else that Paul would have found appealing about Roger Lunn: The man had a kind of intuitive sense about jeans and what they represented to the people who wore them. As far as Lunn was concerned, putting on a pair of jeans was like slipping into a person's own memories. To Lunn, jeans were like rock and roll: Put on a pair of Landlubber bells that you had bought on the King's Road twenty years ago, and suddenly you were back in London in the summer of 1965, and the mod scene was at its zenith.

Paul liked insights like that. He liked the idea that jeans could resonate more than mere clothing—that they could evoke the whole history of a person.

He and Lunn had discussed the idea several times, and by now Paul had begun to visualize what he wanted: a scene in the desert, something haunting and image-laden and full of hot, dusty grit, with nothing around but cactus, sage, and the occasional cattle skulls. It wasn't even a scene, in fact, but an evocation of a mood. The mood had been with him for years, since he'd first sat through the final wild moments of John Huston's *The Misfits*. Over and over he would see the moment replay itself, as Clark Gable and Montgomery Clift roped the wild mustangs, and Marilyn Monroe struggled and pleaded to set them free. What it was about that moment that captivated him so, Paul never understood. The movie was pretentious and boring, but there at the end was something fantastical yet real, perhaps stirring images of his earliest years in North Africa—the dust and wind, the cloudless blue sky that faded to yellow at the horizon. So maybe he had hired Lunn and come four hundred miles into the Arizona desert simply to recapture the moment. With Paul, who could tell?

According to the storyboard, a beat-up 1950s pickup truck would approach from the left and cross, leaving a trail of dust, then disappear. That was it, nothing more, the ultimate minimalist statement. This was Anne Tyler and Georgia O'Keeffe and Werner Fassbinder all rolled into one, and the amazing thing was, it was going to be a commercial —like none ever before seen on television. That was because Paul's commercial wasn't going to sell jeans at all; it was going to sell the feeling that Paul had experienced watching *The Misfits*—seeing Marilyn

Monroe all dusty and voluptuous and vulnerable, out in the desert somewhere with nothing but wild horses and wild men stampeding around her.

Soon the shooting would be over, and the crew would begin packing to leave. Yet back in the editing room this scene would acquire an unforgettable eeriness. At the end of the scene the truck would simply vanish into the desert. Replacing it on the screen would be the company's logo—a downward-pointing triangular patch bearing the word "Guess" with a question mark.

Paul had sketched the logo years earlier, almost on a whim. From the beginning it had held a teasing fascination for him—suggesting, if not to him personally, then to others like Lunn, a quality almost of black magic. Indeed, though Paul may not have realized it even then, the pubic-shaped patch eerily recalls that magical old Aramaic word "abracadabra" of Jewish folklore, which is spelled out—also in the shape of a downward-pointing triangle—to be meditated upon as an amulet in times of danger and stress.

Yet in his way, Paul too seemed to appreciate the patch's power, for now it was to be presented, almost in conjurerlike fashion, as the climax to Guess's television debut. The risks in the commercial were huge, and the costs enormous—the company had budgeted $2 million for air time, and the money would buy them only two weeks' worth of network spots. Yet if the message worked, Guess's business could explode, and by next year $2 million might seem like little more than madmoney.

His brothers hadn't liked the idea—just as they'd been against the deal with the Nakashes. But Paul had been adamant. The time to act was now. An opportunity was at hand, and if they didn't seize it, it might not come again. Gloria Vanderbilt was history, so was Sassoon, so was Sergio Valente. As Paul saw things, it was down to a three-way race—Calvin Klein and Jordache and, coming up fast on the outside, Guess. Soon those other two could be eating Guess's dust. In Paul's view, the Calvin Klein image was too "gay" to go much farther, and as for those Israeli gangsters, the Nakashes . . . well, what could one say? By now Jordache jeans were turning up on construction workers at fifteen dollars a pop. They weren't status-anything anymore, just cardboard-stiff dungarees that sold everywhere at a discount.

As Paul sized things up, the jeans market of tomorrow could belong to Guess. The trick was to establish the brand nationally, establish Georges as a fashion trendsetter. And somewhere deep within him,

Paul seemed to realize that he held the key: his sixty seconds of quick-cut, spare images, all shot in black and white and spliced together to suggest the Southwest as a land of raw power, mystery, and seductive appeal.

Perhaps he could see it even then: The commercial coming on at the tag-end of prime time, just before people snapped off their sets and went to bed—and all over America folks would be trundling down the hall in their bathrobes and slippers and turning to each other and saying, "Hon, what the hell *was* that commercial anyway? You know, the one where they ask you to guess at the end. What was the question? Do you get a prize or something? Next time it comes on, get a pencil and jot it down, will you?"

It was a commercial that mirrored Paul himself: unforgettable, unusual, enigmatic to the core. Paul had even given the company its oddly questioning name.

"I wanted a name that no one would forget," he later told an interviewer. "Something that asked and answered its own question all at once."

What drove him the way it did was a mystery even to Paul. Though he was neither an officer, a director, or even an employee of Guess, by the summer of 1985 he was not only overseeing virtually all of Guess's litigation, but personally handling its advertising and promotion as well.

"Look," said Maurice, "it has been a fact all along that Paul was the one who was running Guess."

Since all four brothers lived within a few blocks of one another, soon all were being collected in Paul's limo each morning for the trip downtown to Guess's corporate offices, located in a one-story brick building at 1714 South Maple Street. It was just another of Paul's "take control" touches.

The company had come a long way since the brothers had left France three years earlier. For Guess's first advertising spread, Paul had hired a local photographer and taken a girl from one of the stores, and piled them into his 1978 Rabbit convertible. Then they'd driven out to Laguna Beach and shot scenes among the rocks and sand. Paul liked the way the girl's long blonde hair became tousled and matted, but as the day progressed he began to feel that she still seemed too stilted and posed. So he rubbed some sand and dirt on her clothing, and it gave her the earthy, sensual look he'd been after.

Soon, a Laguna Beach police car pulled up and a policeman asked if they had a permit to shoot on public property. They didn't, so the police told them to leave. They started packing up as if to do just that, but when the police drove off, the group piled back into the Rabbit and drove down the beach in the opposite direction, then set up to shoot all over again.

The cat-and-mouse game went on for the rest of the day, and when the resulting ads started appearing, people would come up to Paul and remark admiringly not just on the clever gimmick of promoting fashion wear by covering it with dust and dirt, but on the variety of backdrops and settings used for the spreads. Paul would smile appreciatively, never revealing that the only reason there had been such variety was that he and his crew had spent the entire day dodging the cops in order to shoot without a permit.

Since then, Guess's ads had become an increasingly familiar addition to the pages of magazines like *Vanity Fair, Esquire,* and *New York,* even as the company's jeans began turning up in stores like Bloomingdale's. Sales, meanwhile, had taken off, as young people clamored for the skin-tight look of the jeans with the zippered cuffs.

Paul resented claims by the Nakashes that it had been their marketing expertise and management know-how that had made Guess a success. As far as he was concerned, the Nakashes really hadn't done anything —anything, that is, except steal Guess's designs while entangling the company in a Hong Kong tax fraud. The real reason for Guess's success —as anyone could plainly see—was Paul's advertising, and insinuating anything else made him boil with anger.

The Nakash! Paul would sometimes say, lumping them together in his mind as a kind of monolithic force of evil. What were they really but Syrian rug merchants? Indeed, the way he spoke of them would call to mind stories of such people—of how, when the setting sun hit their carpets at just the right angle, the cloth would shimmer in gold and ochre and no price would seem too high to pay. But come the morning, the sun would hit the carpet through the opposite window and the real rug would reveal itself, all moth-eaten and worn—and during the night the rug merchant would have packed up and left for Damascus, and not even the Syrian *muhabarat* would be able to find him.

In a few weeks' time, Paul would have to sit down with the Nakashes all over again. It would be the latest monthly meeting of the Guess board of directors. The Marciano lawsuit to recover their stock was still in the earliest stages of pretrial discovery. But the animosities it had stirred up had already so thoroughly poisoned relations between the parties that conducting board-level business at Guess had become all but impossible. As a result, the presiding judge in the case had appointed a retired colleague from the California Court of Appeals to serve as a tiebreaking seventh member of the board—to prevent the company from being destroyed by the very people fighting for its control.

The next meeting would be the man's first, and years later Paul could still relive the anticipation he apparently felt even then—hoping not simply for stability to return to the board meetings, but for the new appointee to see for himself how nasty and venal the Nakashes really were. All the man had to do was to attend one single meeting. With his own eyes he'd be able to witness the bullying and trickery that the Nakashes were passing off as management of a business.

Chapter 5

In a hotel room in Mexico City, a Latin businessman spoke sadly of corruption with a visitor from Panama. It seemed that wherever one looked in Mexico these days, it was simply impossible to do business without crossing a few palms. The shame of the Republic, the businessman was saying—as, in fact, he'd been saying to his cousin, Mexico's *presidente,* Miguel de la Madrid, only just the other day.

Suitably impressed, the Panamanian visitor nodded in agreement. Then, both men having completed their genuflections before the God of Hypocrisy as required in Latin business affairs, they at last got down to cases—which happened to be some corrupt plans of their own. It seemed the businessman possessed a contract to construct a pipeline across Panama—a pipeline that would compete with a recently completed pipeline that already spanned the isthmus nation.

As the businessman explained to his visitor, the idea behind the new venture was to undercut the existing pipeline and drive it out of business. The financial backing was all in place, the banks had signed on, and all that was needed was some on-site managerial expertise. Which was where the visitor came in.

The visitor had held a top managerial position on the last pipeline project, and as the businessman pointed out, he thus possessed the kind of expertise that would help make the new venture a success. There was just one thing.

"Look," said the businessman, his eyes perhaps narrowing to communicate the seriousness of what was now to follow. "If we are going into business together, I am going to get my 15 percent. I do not know how you Panamanians do it, but I want to have my piece."

"But of course," said the visitor reassuringly. "That is standard."

"Good," said the businessman. "Now how do you propose we work it out?"

It was all very simple, answered the Panamanian, he would handle it the same way he handled the last pipeline . . . and thereupon proceeded to spell out in detail exactly how the kickbacks were structured in the previous deal—structured so that none of the investors in the project would know they were being robbed.

"Then it is done," said the businessman. "We have a deal," and he extended his hand.

Yet the deal was not what the Panamanian thought. For scarcely had the door closed behind the departed visitor than the Mexican was checking the concealed tape recorder that had captured the conversation. The story about his being a cousin of the president of Mexico? A fraud. The contracts and documents he'd used to impress his visitor? All phony. In fact, virtually everything he'd said since the Panamanian had set foot in his room had been a lie.

In reality, the Latin businessman wasn't a businessman at all. He was a private investigator—and onetime paid informant for the Central Intelligence Agency—named Octavio Pena. And he didn't live in Latin America either, but in the distinctly unexotic community of Fort Lee, New Jersey.

Because Pena spoke English, and knew his way around Mexico—and because he had a friend at the New York law firm of Paul, Weiss, Rifkind, Wharton & Garrison—Pena had been hired to set up what amounted to a sting operation in behalf of Northville Industries, the company that owned the original pipeline. The objective of the sting was to see if millions in cost overruns sustained by Northville on the project had been caused by mere mismanagement or perhaps by fraud and thievery by employees on the scene.

The assignment might have seemed daunting for a small-time operator like Pena. In many respects he was little more than a one-man band. His company, which bore the grand-sounding name of Lynch International, was really scarcely more than a mom-and-pop security guard service, employing just over a dozen guards.

Yet what he lacked in bureaucratic bulk he made up for in energy and guile. His contact at Paul, Weiss—one of New York's leading law firms—helped. Private investigators, it is sometimes said, are the surgical gloves that lawyers slip on before performing proctologic examinations on their opponents. And according to Pena, over the years

Paul, Weiss had used him more than once to keep from dirtying its fingers.

Pena's usefulness came from what he was willing to do. Unable to compete toe to toe with such larger firms as Kroll Associates, Pena needed to offer more than merely the ability to pore over a firm's books and records in search of hidden frauds. Accountants could do that anyway. When the accountants and lawyers had all thrown up their hands in defeat and said, "Well, it looks like the guy was just too clever for us," that was when Pena stood ready to help. His basic tactic: to worm his way into the confidence of the suspect and seduce him into committing his crimes all over again.

Sometimes Pena could wrap up a case in a few days or weeks, other times his schemes would drag on for months. It was risky work indeed, for it could put Pena in situations that suggested entrapment and the agent provocateur. But Pena survived by knowing just how far he could go, and in the end his stratagems almost always got results. Over the years, he'd caught crooked employees for clients by sometimes actually involving low-level federal agents in his plots. Doing so not only assured the client that criminal charges would be brought against the suspect in the end, but also protected Pena from being blamed as a coconspirator if the sting didn't work.

To his neighbors in Fort Lee, Pena was the very model of an unassuming family man, and he could often be seen playing catch in the afternoon with one or the other of his two children in front of the former church rectory that he'd bought years earlier and that now served as his office. The children attended parochial school, the wife lent a hand at the office, and in the springtime forsythia bushes blossomed around the rectory to round out the picture of tranquility.

But nothing in Pena's life was what it appeared to be, from the bushy black hairpiece that reportedly hid decade-old scars sustained in a nearly fatal auto accident, to the musty and unprepossessing church rectory that in fact housed room after room of case files, terminals and computer wire, and tapes—the results of more than twenty years of lying and deceiving as a way of life. When he left town on assignment, Pena could be wearing cowboy boots and a leather jacket, or a double-breasted mohair and monogrammed shirts. Speaking with an accent that could have been learned anywhere from Puerto Rico to Haifa, Pena might have been a banker from Brazil, or he might have been a businessman from Alexandria.

In reality, he had been born in Mexico City in 1941, the son of a

Mexican lawyer and a mother from Philadelphia. Though not grandly wealthy, the Penas were well-off—or so Pena liked to claim—not least thanks to real estate holdings on the mother's side of the family in Philadelphia.

The Pena family lived in Mexico City's Polanco district, an area of sidewalks and haciendas, where many of the country's leading government officials and business people maintained homes. Or so Pena said. Next door to the Penas was the home of Mexico's minister of defense, General Urquizo, and nearby were the homes of other important figures. Or so he would say.

Yet it was the American side of his lineage that most fascinated Octavio. For one thing, it seemed that whenever his parents got into a discussion over something they did not want Octavio to overhear, they slipped into English to discuss it. To the curious youngster, it was as if English were the language of mystery and secrets—the realm to which even his own parents retreated in times of need.

But there was more, for by the 1940s and early 1950s, economic nationalism had already begun to take root in Mexico. And as Octavio could see with his own eyes every day—indeed, as he could hear repeated by his mother at the dinner table every night—it was in *el norte* that the future held promise, not in Mexico with its dirt roads, starving mestizos, and angry college students.

Like a youngster who collects baseball cards, Octavio began collecting American mannerisms. He begged his parents to have hot dog cookouts on the weekends. He became known in the neighborhood and at school as "Admiral America." To Pena, the colossus to the north wasn't a threat to his nation, it represented its salvation.

In the late 1950s, Pena entered the University of Mexico City, intent upon studying law. But it was a time when the campus was increasingly in the grip of leftist agitators, and student radicals were everywhere. Before he quite realized what was happening, Pena was spying on them for the U.S. Embassy.

"I was very popular, and people would tell me everything," Pena declared later.

Soon the CIA, which operated under diplomatic cover in the embassy, had recruited Pena as a paid informant. In 1961, at the age of twenty-one, he was sent by the Agency to Miami. This was in the immediate aftermath of the Bay of Pigs, and Miami was seething with angry anti-Castro Cubans who felt they'd been betrayed by Washington. Pena's assignment, which lasted eleven months, was to infiltrate one of the groups, which operated "Radio Swan," an anti-Castro radio station, and report on its plans.

"All the anti-Castro guys were actually extortionists and drug dealers," Pena later reported. "Many were CIA operatives. Some threw bombs to shake down auto dealers."

In the late 1960s Pena turned up in New York. He had money in his pocket, but he spoke no English. He answered a classified ad for an "investigator," was interviewed for the position by a man named "Jerry," and by a fluke wound up as the office manager, at ninety-five dollars a week, in the moribund New York office of Lynch & Company, a Midwest-based detective agency that had fallen on hard times.

Pena's first case was in Newark, New Jersey. A subsidiary of the 3M Corporation was missing large quantities of Scotch Tape. "I went undercover, and within weeks I had cracked the case," Pena declared. "I found it very exciting."

To drum up more work, Pena bought some Savile Row business suits, had business cards printed up describing himself as "ex-FBI and CIA," and began going up and down the office blocks of midtown Manhattan, walking into offices and leaving his card on desks.

"One of my first clients was Paul, Weiss," Pena recalled. Another was Borden & Company, also in midtown.

"Somehow I got in to see the chairman, Mr. Marusi," Pena declared. "He asked me, 'Do you investigate stolen typewriters?' and I said sure! So he send me to a vice-president named Charlie. Eventually I put on jeans and start speaking Spanish with people. This way I find out it was the guards and security people doing the stealing. Out of that Mr. Marusi give me the guard concession. I went out and bought uniforms, patches, everything. I wound up hiring off-duty cops. Later I find a refugee placement office and I get plenty of Romanians too. It was like hiring the Foreign Legion."

One case led to the next, and eventually Pena was moving into more shadowy pursuits. He was being hired to recover the kidnapped children of Chinese millionaires (or so he would claim). He was being asked to crack Latin-American dope rings for the Drug Enforcement Administration (or so he would say). In one case that did get a fair amount of attention, he turned up working for Pepsico, in cooperation with IRS agents in Dallas, to break up a ring of Pepsico executives who were using the firm's Frito-Lay corn chips subsidiary in an international tax scam.

Then came his biggest case of all, as Pena took on the Mafia itself—

or at least a Long Island gasoline bootlegger named Lawrence Iorizzo who had ties to the Colombo family. The assignment came by way of a Long Island bankruptcy court, which had been unable to track down some money that Iorizzo had hidden abroad before himself becoming a fugitive from justice. Eventually the assignment wound up with Pena. To help him, Pena hired a former FBI agent named Sally Godfrey, who had a background in sex crimes and homicide investigations. Together, they discovered where the money was hidden, and as icing on the cake Pena even managed, free of charge, to lure Iorizzo into a trap set by the FBI to capture the thug.

It's what Pena would do—make friends with gangsters, then give them up to the government.

If Pena was beginning to get a swelled head, well who could really blame him? In a day or so he'd be returning to New York, and he could no doubt see the outcome already. The accused executives would holler and protest, and claim that they'd been tricked. But in the end the tapes would speak for themselves. There would undoubtedly be some heated negotiations, probably in a neutral place like the Waldorf-Astoria. But when the doors swung open and the men walked out, the client would have its money back, the embezzlers would be headed for jail, and Pena would never have stepped from the shadows. He was Tezcatlipoca, the Aztec god of smoke and mirrors, whose roving eye saw all the earth and heavens at once—farther even than Michtlantecutli, who appears as the owl and is lord of the midnight hour.

Now, with yet another triumph at hand, Pena no doubt wondered what new assignment would come his way next. What new snake would slither across the path of Octavio Pena, operative extraordinaire?

Chapter 6

In a world as ingrown and clubby as the New York corporate legal community, people were forever unexpectedly bumping into one another on cases. Sometimes conflicts of interest were inescapable and obvious, and in such circumstances, professional ethics required one party or the other to declare itself "conflicted out" of the case, or at least to obtain a waiver from the client stating that continued representation was okay.

Yet the practice of corporate law was also a business, and in the "sue me" 1980s, the players were learning to tolerate moves that might have seemed less acceptable at an earlier time. Just as generals and admirals would retire from the Pentagon only to turn up as lobbyists and executives for defense contractors, assistant prosecutors from the Southern District were forever stepping down from government after three or four years, only to reemerge as litigating partners in big corporate law firms they had only recently opposed.

Legally, there was usually nothing wrong with such arrangements, but they did add a level of complexity to relationships, as people needed to stay on guard against a misstep or slip of the tongue that might get them conflicted out of the game.

One of the firms most adept at navigating these hazards was Kroll Associates. Companies and law firms alike sought Kroll's services—for investigating opponents in takeover fights, for probing the weaknesses of witnesses and evidence in law suits—in fact, for just about any form of business world conflict in which information could bring advantage to the side that possessed it. Lately, Kroll had even begun to emerge as a potent new button-pusher in the power politics of the Southern District.

Taking their cue from the founder of the firm, Jules Kroll, a salty-tongued former assistant prosecutor in the Manhattan district attorney's office, Kroll people liked to tell clients that when it came to dealing with the feds, the folks at Kroll knew exactly how to make things happen. They might not be able to get a case killed, but they could certainly get a client's side of the story whispered in the right ears. Likewise, they'd say, if a client had a complaint to lodge against a business competitor, or maybe one of its own employees, Kroll Associates could see to it that the feds at least gave the matter a fair hearing. In this way, contacts made in one case—often relatively low-level assistant prosecutors or investigators—became "confidential sources" in the next, as the firm's mystique for being "plugged in" just grew and grew.

One such case involved Warner-Lambert Pharmaceuticals in New Jersey, and the connections that it created for both Kroll and Bruce Dollar were surprising to say the least. The case began toward the summer of 1985, not long after the Marcianos had handed over Dollar's dossier on the Nakashes to Ron Saranow in Los Angeles.

Warner-Lambert was a big player in drugs and brand-name household products, and also happened to make Chiclets brand chewing gum. As a result, near-pandemonium erupted at Warner-Lambert headquarters when the phone rang one day and it was the chairman of archrival Wrigley's Gum on the other end, calling from Chicago to reveal that he'd just been approached by a man offering to sell him trade secrets from Warner-Lambert's own files.

Once they regained their composure, the people at Warner-Lambert turned to Kroll: Could the super-snoops help ferret out the rat's identity?

Bruce Dollar and Bart Schwartz got the case, and one look at the facts suggested a devilish idea: Why not try a sting operation!

The Wrigley chairman agreed to cooperate. Secret telephone taping is illegal in Illinois, so if the Warner-Lambert man ever called back, the Wrigley man promised to refer him to Dollar in New York. Then Dollar, with a tape recorder at the ready, would record the conversation and try to set up a face-to-face meeting.

The man did call back, and just as agreed, he was referred to Dollar —who of course identified himself not as a Kroll private eye but rather as a Wrigley executive who'd been authorized to conduct negotiations for the trade secrets. A rendezvous was set for a Manhattan restaurant, and at the appointed hour, there Dollar sat, wearing a hidden body microphone, as Schwartz and other Kroll operatives lurked at nearby tables as eyewitnesses to the transaction.

The luncheon went off without a hitch, and with tape in hand, the operatives went back to the office to figure out what to do with it. One possibility was simply to turn the incriminating evidence over to Warner-Lambert, collect their fee, and be done with it. In fact, a normal investigation by private eyes would have ended right there. But the folks at Kroll thought of themselves as more than simply normal PIs—they were "full-service" investigators, a cut above the rest, who could not only dig up the dirt, but get the government to act on it.

So it didn't take long before the two men decided to get the U.S. Attorney's Office involved. Not only would Kroll's fee jump accordingly, but Kroll would simultaneously be making a deposit in the favor bank of good relations with the folks downtown.

As luck would have it, the chief outside counsel for Warner-Lambert was John Martin, Giuliani's predecessor as head of the Southern District. With Martin and Schwartz *together* behind the case, there seemed little doubt that the Southern District would be willing to take it on.

The question was, Who should it be offered to? Was this a "Big Crimes" matter or a "Little Crimes" matter? And in either case, who would be most appreciative of being handed what amounted to prima facie proof of theft and mail fraud targeted against a *Fortune* 500 company? Who, in short, would be in the best position to return the favor by helping Kroll out with any other irons it might have in the fires of the Southern District? The folks at Kroll could only hope for the best.

One thing led to another, and shortly thereafter the case was dropped in the lap of the Major Crimes Unit chief at the time, a fellow named Barry Bohrer. Bohrer in turn looked around to see who in his already-overworked group could handle just one more case, and by and by his eye fell upon the bright young associate who'd just finished up as second chair on the Black Liberation Army case—Lorna Schofield.

Almost immediately thereafter, Barry Bohrer left the government for private practice, and a new man took over as unit chief. His name was Marty Perschetz, and he scarcely knew Lorna Schofield at all, let alone that she'd recently been given a case from Dollar and Schwartz that involved Warner-Lambert. Thus, he had no way of knowing, in the wake of the meeting with Schwartz and the others six week later in Wilson's office, that to give the Jordache tax case to Schofield would be to burden her with yet another Kroll-generated case—and from the same two men, Dollar and Schwartz.

But the folks at Kroll knew that all too well, and as far as they were concerned, it must have been a dream come true. After all, it now suddenly looked as if eager young Lorna Schofield would be prosecuting not just one Kroll-inspired case at a time but two! Meanwhile, just offstage, the snoops in wing tips would have made their deepest penetration yet into the world of the Southern District—even as they collected their fees while simultaneously bolstering their reputation as the biggest button-pushers in the game.

Chapter 7

It was November of 1985, and the mood of Thanksgiving hung in the air as the IRS's chief criminal investigator in Los Angeles, Ron Saranow, stepped from his fifth-floor office at the Federal Building to keep a luncheon appointment. Though his Japanese-born secretary, Kumi, maintained Saranow's records and files, Ron kept track of his own appointments.

Ron liked to think of himself as a cool number, the sort of man who had things under control. Yet on this particular day he'd apparently been swept by the kind of foolish excitement that comes from reckless entanglements, wantonly pursued. In the fables of Aesop, there's plenty of room for mischief between flattery and self-delusion, and like the lover who believes she's desired for her mind alone, Saranow didn't seem to have been thinking straight for weeks.

Passing by Kumi's desk he headed straight for the elevator, a sense of anticipation perhaps quickening his stride. He was off for lunch—not with a woman other than his wife, but with his captivating new friend in the jeans business, Paul Marciano. They were going to a restaurant in the apparel mart, and Ron had been told that Paul would be waiting for him with a car on the street below.

In the gossipy world of the CID, where spying on colleagues seemed to take up as much time as spying on tax cheats, "Saranow and the Marcianos" was already becoming a hot topic at the water cooler. But what did Saranow care? Looking back on the time years later, he explained that being the target of office gossip was unavoidable for a man in his position.

True enough, for it was the power of his office, and the manner in which he wielded that power, that made Ron Saranow an object of gossip and fascination. On an IRS organizational chart, Saranow's operation would have appeared as but one of sixty-three criminal divisions, all of them overshadowed by dozens of other innocuous-sounding divisions, ranging from Computer Services to Program Planning and Review Staff. But the IRS's CID troops were the Waffen SS of the Service, their mere existence serving to encourage compliance with the nation's bewilderingly complex tax laws.

Moreover, as a nearly twenty-year veteran of the IRS, Saranow belonged to an old-boy network of similarly long-serving CID men, who all now held top management posts around the country. Wherever one looked, Saranow had friends. Saranow was said to have friends in the CID offices of Chicago, Atlanta, Cincinnati, Dallas, San Francisco, New York, and other cities.

It was the very scope of these friendships—and the rumors they spawned of Saranow as an incorrigible string-puller—that kept the rumor mills turning. Some of his colleagues lionized him as a go-for-broke chief investigator who was totally committed to his work; others reviled him as a self-aggrandizing power seeker and schemer. Saranow's friend's would defend him as the best chief criminal investigator in the IRS; Saranow's enemies would whisper that he was an office Lothario. There was even at least one rumor—though seemingly baseless—that tied Saranow to underworld crime figures in Chicago, citing as evidence that he had allegedly once been granted a ten-thousand-dollar line of credit at the Mob-linked Stardust Hotel.

Yet if Saranow was beginning to sense more eyes than ever upon him, it would not have been hard to guess why: his increasingly open involvement with the Marcianos. No doubt he could imagine what the folks were saying when he wasn't around: Marcianos? Nice Sicilian-sounding name. And from Marseilles to boot!

In fact, when it came to the Marcianos, Saranow was no longer sure quite what he felt. On the one hand, he had wanted to keep everything clean and straight and not send out mixed signals. On the other hand, well, what could he say? So maybe the Marcianos were really rich. And maybe they did live in Beverly Hills. And maybe they did have so many Bentleys and Lincolns parked in their driveways that you sometimes couldn't get in or out.

The thing was, strip away all that superficial stuff—all the glamour and wealth and fashion industry prestige—and when you got right down to it, Georges and Maurice and Armand and Paul were really just four guys named Joe. So down-to-earth and real. So much like Ron. So right on his wavelength.

Perhaps there was a bit of self-delusion in all this. But if so, it was understandable. After all, there he was, Ron Saranow, a seventy-two-thousand-dollar-a-year civil servant two years from retirement, and what did he have to show for it? Really not all that much. All his life Saranow had loved sports cars. But now, with retirement looming before him, did he have a Lamborghini, or a Ferrari Testarossa, or even a Porsche Carrera? What he had was a wife and house in the Valley, and a daughter who'd married someone in the Highway Patrol—and any day now his boss would be getting reassigned, maybe even to London, and Ron wouldn't be moving up to take over.

That was when the Marcianos had turned up—steered as if by some guiding hand right into Saranow's life. Saranow's first meeting with them back in the spring had taken place in a fifth-floor conference room, just down the hall from his office. Saranow had been summoned to the room by his boss, District Director Bill Connett, who'd given him no indication of the purpose of the meeting, or who would be there, but had simply asked that he attend.

In the room Saranow had found Connett and two strangers. One was introduced to him as Paul Marciano, an apparel industry business-man, and the other as Gary Iskowitz, a former IRS official who now worked as Marciano's accountant. As best Saranow could make out, Iskowitz and Connett were friends of long standing, and it appeared that Iskowitz had used that relationship to arrange the get-together.

Formalities finished, the meeting got down to specifics. It seemed that the Marcianos were suing a Los Angeles businessman named Boh-bot. He was a Guess licensee who'd allegedly been manufacturing denim jeans with Guess labels, but selling the goods for cash off his factory's back loading dock and not paying the Marcianos the royalties they were entitled to receive.

Why tell the IRS? Because, explained Iskowitz, the way that Bohbot was allegedly cheating on his license meant that he was probably si-multaneously cheating on his taxes. As proof, Iskowitz placed a binder of documents on the table. It was all there, he explained—as clear a case of tax fraud as Connett and Saranow were likely to encounter in a long time.

The meeting lasted about an hour, and after it ended Saranow took the documents and gave them to an assistant named Phil, who in turn passed them on to a subordinate named Al, who shoved them even further down the ladder. Later, Saranow said he had given the matter little thought. In a given week, dozens of cases crossed his desk, and this one wasn't yet even a case.

Yet several days later, Connett stuck his head in Saranow's office with more news from the two tipsters. It seemed that the French one with the accent—Marciano—had invited Connett and Saranow to a meeting at his home in Beverly Hills. Marciano apparently wanted to blow the whistle on yet another group of people he was suing.

Perhaps Saranow should have been more mindful of the vengeful and jealous motives that usually drive people to become IRS informants in the first place. But in this case he wasn't. And his fascination with his new garment industry tipster must surely have increased as he pulled to a stop at number 616 Roxbury Drive, high in the canyons of Beverly Hills. Saranow's own modest home sat only ten miles away, but in another economic reality altogether, behind a boxwood hedge at the end of a cul-de-sac in the San Fernando Valley community of Tarzana. Yet here before him stood a sprawling Tudor estate approached by a circular drive and shaded by palms. It was grand.

It was at this meeting that Saranow was tipped to the case against the Nakashes, once again being provided with a professionally packaged binder of supporting documents and photographs. As with the Bohbot file, this one had also been prepared by Kroll Associates, and came complete with thumb-tabs for easy leafing.

No one in Saranow's office understood much about how the garment industry worked. But Paul wasn't about to let that stop him. Six months earlier, Saranow would not have known the man from a stranger on a street corner. By now, Paul had become almost an auxiliary IRS agent. The case against the Nakashes had been passed on to New York, but the Bohbot matter had remained in L.A. And every day Saranow would come to work and barely get his coat off before the phone would ring and it would be Paul on the other end offering advice and guidance on how to hunt down Bohbot.

Soon, Marciano's calls were going not only to Saranow but to virtually every subordinate Ron had assigned to the case. Paul had tips and advice for them all—on where to look for hidden cash, how to read the secret meanings in seemingly straightforward transactions. It was as if the L.A. office were being given a guided tour through the tax fraud hells of the entire garment industry—and only the Marcianos could lead the way.

Meanwhile, something else seemed to be happening as well. Saranow couldn't put his finger on quite when it began, but in some way that seemed to defy precise description, the terms of his relationship with Marciano had begun ever so subtly to change.

In fact, the more Saranow thought about it, the more he realized it was true: He and Paul were actually becoming friends. It was apparently no longer simply Paul and Ron, informant and IRS agent; now it was Ron Saranow, wise old government executive, and Paul Marciano, eager young businessman feeling his oats. In fact, whenever the two men got together, they often wouldn't talk about Bohbot or the Nakashes at all, but about the general business affairs of Guess instead. It was as if the IRS's top criminal investigator in L.A. had become one of the oddest business lunch tax deductions in IRS history—a write-off for his own informant.

Lately, Saranow had begun to sense the ripening of the most beguiling possibility of all. In some subtle and vague way (if such words could *ever* be applied to Paul), the young Marciano seemed to be sizing Saranow up as—dare he say it?—potential Guess executive material!

It wasn't as if Marciano had actually come right out and offered Saranow a job. The two had spoken many times since the Marcianos had first walked through his door in the spring of 1985, and the subject of a job offer had never come up once. It was just that, well, every time Saranow spoke to Paul the man seemed to find a way to bring up how fast Guess was growing, and how overworked everyone was, and how impossible it was to keep track of everything.

Paul was like a broken record on the subject: Ron, it's really serious, he'd say; we've simply got to find a hands-on guy to help us run the show around here—someone we trust and are comfortable with. You understand. As Paul would stress, the man didn't even need a background in garment making, the brothers could teach him all of that. What they needed was someone with experience at managing large numbers of people, someone who could crack the whip, make the trains run on time.

No wonder the Marcianos had captured his fancy. Maybe they didn't realize it, but they were talking about *him!* So what if his sum total of fashion industry knowledge consisted of what he'd picked up from Paul about how to cheat on taxes. Those Marciano boys obviously knew management talent when they saw it.

A few weeks earlier Saranow had flown to San Francisco with a group of CID colleagues for a week of management lectures. What he thought, day after day in those management lectures, isn't known even to this day. But it's a fair bet he thought a lot about that glamour business down in Beverly Hills—that business the Marcianos apparently wanted him to join and shape up.

Thus it came to pass, toward the end of the lectures, that Saranow and some subordinates had headed over to an IRS hangout known as the Balboa Café. It was just after 5:00 P.M., and the place was as noisy and busy as ever. A table by the front window was empty, so they took it. Drinks were ordered, and everyone settled in.

Several of the group who'd flown up from L.A. were at the table. Where the rest were, Saranow didn't know. And perhaps he didn't much care. Saranow wanted out! And suddenly he was saying so, right out loud, to the person sitting next to him at the table, his voice carrying over the din of the Balboa Café happy-hour crowd.

"It looks like I'm going to be getting an early out," he was boasting. "A kind of leave-without-pay situation. Going to work for the Marcianos. Six-figure salary, complete with a car . . ."

Later, Saranow said he could barely remember who he had been talking to back there in the Balboa Café, let alone who else might have been at the table. Yet now, as he stepped from the Federal Building into the noonday winter glare, there was the future—a black Cadillac limousine, idling at curbside, and inside: Paul Marciano.

As the door clicked shut behind him and the limousine eased into the flow of traffic, Saranow felt a sense of embarrassment and discomfort. What was he doing being picked up in a limo by his own informant? It didn't look right.

Yet it is not given—even to all-knowing, all-seeing IRS criminal investigators—to hear the cackling of the *Jinn* as they plot and conspire to bring misery to men. And that is too bad, for even as Saranow stepped into the waiting Guess limousine, five stories above street level in the window of an IRS office with a clear view of the street below, an IRS criminal investigator stared down in disbelief.

The Olympian observer was a Saranow subordinate named Phil Xanthos, who only days earlier had sat at that table in San Francisco's Balboa Café and overheard his boss blurt out the news that he was quitting the IRS to go to work for the Marcianos. Listening to what Saranow had announced, Xanthos could scarcely believe his ears; the man was going to take a job working for his own tipsters?

Now, standing at the window of IRS headquarters, Xanthos couldn't believe his eyes either, as Saranow stepped brazenly from the Federal Building straight into a waiting Guess limousine—for lunch with his own informant and future employer, Paul Marciano.

Chapter 8

On a crisp morning that November, a dignified-looking man with close-cropped, curly hair and a heavyset frame stepped from his car and approached a two-story brick building in downtown Los Angeles. The man was Richard Schauer, sixty-three, retired chief judge of the California Court of Appeals, and the building contained the executive offices of Guess. The address was hardly Rodeo Drive—wedged as it was between the Santa Monica and Harbor freeways—but Schauer probably didn't expect to be visiting the place all that often anyway. Schauer was beginning a new postretirement career as the court-appointed provisional director—and tiebreaking seventh member—of the Guess Inc. board of directors. And today was to be the first board meeting of the company at which he would preside.

A steady and even-tempered man, Schauer tried to keep an open mind about things. Now, that quality would be more important than ever, for judging from what he'd heard and read of the case already, the owners of this company hardly seemed to be overflowing with fellow feeling for one another.

That August, Schauer had been selected by his longtime friend and former colleague on the California bench, Superior Court Judge Norman Epstein, to join the Guess board. As Epstein had explained the situation, Guess was in the apparel business—specifically the manufacture of so-called designer jeans—and it was fast becoming one of the largest and most important firms in the industry. But the company was jointly owned by two groups of brothers—one of which headed a rival firm in New York, Jordache Enterprises—and the families had been at each other's throats for nearly a year.

Big money was at stake in the fight, and perhaps that alone was reason enough for the backbiting behavior that seemed to be gripping the company. As Schauer understood things, the two groups each owned half the firm, and they were said to quarrel incessantly over every business issue imaginable, from the payment of bonuses to demands for the appointment of a receiver to run the company.

Back and forth the charges had flown, escalating to the point that Epstein had started attacking the two sides in his courtroom for running a kind of war of attrition. If this were allowed to keep up, Epstein had worried, Guess might tear itself apart before the issues in the suit were ever decided.

So to break the impasse, Epstein had decided to appoint a neutral seventh director for the board. Initially, the Nakashes had wanted Epstein to remove the Marcianos entirely—oust them from the board—but the judge had decided not to, arguing that for all their unconscionable behavior, the Marcianos were undeniably making huge amounts of money for the company. Better, he ruled, to interpose a tiebreaking mediator between the two sides.

It was an idea that had met with quick acceptance from Marcianos and Nakashes alike, and for an obvious enough reason: At least this would get the company off dead-center. Besides, bringing in a seventh member was in keeping with one of the more fundamental Halakhic applications of the Talmud itself, which holds that no rabbinical court may be composed of an even number of judges. After all, with such a division, how would one know which side God was really on?

Because he both knew him and respected him, Epstein had turned to Schauer. As the tiebreaking seventh member, Schauer stood to draw a hefty stipend for what was obviously going to be a difficult job, and Epstein could think of no person more deserving of the opportunity.

Yet as Schauer himself would have been the first to admit, he actually knew little about the apparel industry or jeans making. Mainly his expertise had been in appellate litigation, and since his retirement from the bench, in corporate work for the Century City office of Sidley & Austin, the Chicago law firm that numbered AT&T among its corporate clients. But Schauer was widely regarded in California legal circles as a man of high character, steady nerves, and impeccable credentials—exactly the qualities needed for success in the emotion-charged environment in which Epstein had invited him to become, in effect, a referee.

As any good judge would have, Schauer no doubt realized that utter impartiality would be the key to his success. For all he knew, everything the two sides accused each other of could be true. Get drawn into this fight and he might never be seen or heard from again.

To all available evidence, then, that was Schauer's view of the situation as he entered the Guess offices and proceeded into the lobby, looking for someone to greet him. Yet if he harbored any illusions that good intentions alone were what the situation called for, they were dispelled within minutes of having set foot in the door. For scarcely had he been ushered into the Guess boardroom and begun introducing himself to a group of waiting Marciano lawyers than a furious commotion erupted behind him back in the lobby.

Over the din came the shout, "We are the owners of this company, open the door and let us in!"

It was Joe Nakash, the oldest of the three Nakash brothers, along with Avi, Ralph, and a crowd of Jordache lawyers and executives, all trying to shove their way past Paul Marciano and into the boardroom.

"You're here to spy! Get out, get out!" cried Paul, as he pointed and railed at a Jordache vice-president named Goldberg, against whom Paul had been nursing a grudge for months. Having now discovered him at the Guess front door, apparently intent upon attending the first board meeting to be chaired by Schauer, Paul had flown into a rage and began trying to push him back into the street.

This instantly seemed to bring out the most aggressive instincts in Joe Nakash, who, as Paul recounted it later, got behind Goldberg and started trying to push him back inside. Before anyone knew it, Paul and Joe were trading punches, as panicky cries for help rose from all directions. Heads started to pop out of offices, and lawyers rushed from the boardroom, leaving Schauer alone in bewilderment, as if someone had just shouted "Run for your life!" in a tongue that he alone did not understand.

Eventually, the two combatants were pried apart, and with chests heaving and shirttails flapping the group headed back for the boardroom. Yet scarcely had everyone entered and the Nakashes been introduced to Schauer than Avi began demanding that Paul be ejected from the room. This brought a counterdemand from Marshall Grossman, the Marciano lawyer, who insisted that if Paul had to go then so did Goldberg.

Seemingly agog at the bedlam, Schauer ruled that under the circumstances perhaps it would be best if both left.

Humiliated and raging, Paul rose to depart, and how could he have felt otherwise? Here he was, Paul Marciano, the mastermind of the entire Guess strategy, ejected from the boardroom like a shamed school brat while everyone else got to stay behind and fight! Some impression this must be making on Schauer. What if the Nakashes now started to tell him that it had been Paul who'd started the fight! How could Paul even defend himself?

What Paul thought in that instant isn't known even to this day. But what he did most certainly is. According to an old Moroccan proverb, if you can't get in the front door then you try the back window, and moments later Paul was doing just that, as he turned the handle on a side door halfway down the corridor, then slipped into a darkened room. A faint sliver of light could be seen coming from a crack in some bifold doors along the far wall. They were the same bifold doors that opened on to the conference room. Beyond them Paul could hear the voices of the people in the board meeting from which he'd just been expelled.

Listening carefully he could have picked out the slimy mumble of Avi, and hearing it he would have perhaps envisioned the man muttering into his hands while everyone around the table strained to make out what he was saying.

For months Paul had been trying to put the evil eye on Avi. The Nakashes had learned to avoid Paul like a plague, but whenever they were in Los Angeles (which was as little as possible), or whenever Paul was in New York (which nowadays turned out to be all the time thanks to his secret cooperation with the grand jury), Paul would find an opportunity to seek Avi out, get right up close to him, and start to stare.

Now at last it was starting to work; it was beginning to look as if he was actually driving Avi crazy. "Why is he staring at me like that?" Avi would ask. "What did *I* do?" Then when people would turn to see what Avi was talking about, Paul would instantly look away. It was great! He was making Avi nuts. Paul couldn't stand the way the Nakashes, with their Syrian heritage, lorded it over himself and his brothers—how they made a point of looking down on them as dirty Moroccans—never coming right out and saying anything, mind you, simply letting them know by the way they looked, their shifting eyes and sideways glances.

Whether or not he would have put it in so many words, there was but one way to fight back—*Ayin ha-ra,* the evil eye! Yet here he was, at last ready to creep out of the wadi and hurl his biggest zinger yet—and he'd been banished to the kitchen like some shaka-shrouded Bedouin scold, even as the mumbling Nakash got to stay behind and spew forth his blackhearted lies with impunity. It was unspeakable.

Moving carefully in the darkness so as not to knock anything over, he felt his way among some folding tables and an espresso coffee maker until his fingers gripped the back of a chair. Silently he picked it up and tiptoed toward the sliver of light. Then he set the chair down, stealthily eased himself into it, and positioned his eyeball at the crack. It was perfect—an unobstructed view of Avi!—and he began giving the hated Nakash the evil eye all over again.

What Paul may have thought during those silent, spying moments is a mystery. But it's a fair bet he wasn't thinking about how much he liked the people who had just tried to beat him up. In fact, with bickering over nothing going on eight feet away from him, maybe his mind began to drift off to yet another plot he'd lately been working on to make life hell for his tormentors.

To Paul at least, it seemed that every time the Marcianos served a document production order on the Nakashes, the Nakashes would answer by saying that the documents being sought couldn't be produced because they weren't in their possession—they were unfortunately in Hong Kong. Customs orders? They were in Hong Kong. Inflated invoices? Hong Kong. It seemed everything was in Hong Kong.

So Paul was going to see for himself exactly what was in those Jordache files in Hong Kong. He was going to take Grossman and Dollar and reach halfway around the world, and somehow or other do the same thing in Hong Kong that he'd done in New York—that is, stir up the law. Perhaps a smile would have spread across his face at the thought. Avi might have managed to get him expelled from his own boardroom for now, but it wouldn't be long before the wheel of fate would turn. And when it did, Avi would know the meaning of being licked by the tongues of hell.

Suddenly Paul froze. From the other room came the words of Avi.

"Mr. Chairman," he said, pointing toward the bifold doors. "Is there someone behind there? I think Paul Marciano is behind that wall."

In the darkness Paul could hear his heart start to pound. Was he about to be discovered? Would Avi get up and walk over and draw back the door? What would Paul say—"Hi?" It was impossible.

"I do not know," came the voice of Judge Schauer. "But I'd suggest for now that we concern ourselves with events inside this room and not out of it."

Slowly, Paul began to exhale. His secret was safe. And hunching back over he put his eyeball to the crack again and resumed his staring.

Chapter 9

It was just around closing time on a day in that same November of 1985 when Armand Marciano sent Guess's head of production, Cary Nadler, to run an errand. He was to take an accountant from Peat Marwick over to the office of a Guess licensee, Jeff Bohbot, to examine some records.

Nadler knew well enough who Bohbot was: He was the other Marciano enemy—along with the Nakashes—whom Paul and his brothers were suing as well as secretly ratting on to the IRS.

The errand seemed ordinary enough. Yet when it came to the Marcianos you could never tell. The fact was, working for Guess was making Nadler a nervous wreck.

An aging hippie with a ponytail, Nadler managed the day-to-day production operation at Guess's main plant. Long gone were those peace-and-love moods of yesteryear. Thanks to Guess it seemed Cary's life had become an unending series of conflicts and tension. His marriage was falling apart, his brother was sick, and looming over everything was the situation at the office. He was taking five-milligram tablets of Valium to keep control of things, and seeing a therapist to boot, but it wasn't doing any good. How could it? How could he spell out what the people at Guess really had him doing?

According to the doctors, Nadler was suffering from acute anxiety and depression, but what did they know? By now his blood pressure had crept into the 160 range where you started worrying about a power failure. Meanwhile, every day seemed to bring a development that simply nudged the number higher. Just the other day, for example, Nadler had emerged from work to find that Maurice Marciano had backed into Nadler's new Corvette in the parking lot and put a huge dent in the side. Now the driver's-side door wouldn't open and Nadler had to crawl in and out through the passenger side. Nadler didn't want to file a claim with his insurance because his rates were sky-high already, but Maurice had sent Guess's chief financial officer, Bill Merrigan, upstairs to tell him too bad: Nadler would have to cover the claim on his own.

It was the little things like this that were wearing him down. The work was draining enough. The Marcianos paid him well, it was true. In the nearly two years that he'd worked for them he'd received three or four raises already, and was now making eleven hundred dollars a week—which wasn't bad for a San Diego State dropout who lived in Glendale and had been working in the garment industry since high school. But it was what he had to do for that money that had him on edge.

Officially, Nadler's job began where preproduction ended; when fabric was cut into patterns and ready to be sewn together into pants, Nadler took over—and he stayed in control until the completed garments were ready to be shipped.

But the job was impossible. From a standing start three years ago, Guess's business had exploded beyond all belief. By the end of the year, Cary figured the company would have shipped upwards of twenty million garments—for 1985 alone! It was an unheard-of amount, and Cary was the eye of the needle through which it all had to pass. That was the problem. Every time he turned around, the Marcianos had opened a new operation somewhere else in town—washing, cutting, sewing, shipping. And it wasn't just for Guess either. There were all sorts of labels cropping up—a line called "C.O.D.," another called "Panic." To Nadler, the latter must have seemed a perfect name for almost anything that emerged from the chaotically mushrooming world of Guess.

All this was obvious to anyone; Guess had become the hottest apparel house in California, maybe even the country. Yet inside Guess itself was a hidden world in which Nadler had been living a secret double life, and it clearly seemed to be making him sick. He'd talked about it with various people he trusted at the plant, in particular his boss in production, Marcia Knotts.

Knotts's favorite topic was Maurice Marciano.

He was awful, she would say; he screamed and yelled and blew up over nothing. Finally Knotts told Nadler she was meeting with a lawyer from Jordache and was going to quit.

"Watch out," Nadler had warned her. "You could be playing with fire."

But Knotts had gone ahead and met the Jordache lawyer anyway, and told him all about how Maurice would scream at the employees and abuse them, and how hard it was to work for him, and all the other things that were on her mind.

And just as Nadler had feared, the Marcianos had sniffed it out, and hit her with a subpoena, and put her under oath, and started attacking her with questions.

Now Knotts was gone from the company. Yet Nadler was still there, carrying around his desperate little secrets—about the Chinese, and the envelopes, and everything else that he'd gotten himself tangled up in.

Week after week, in would come the Chinese and Korean subcontractors with the envelopes. It's for Abel Eljam, they'd tell him, here. And Nadler would take the envelopes, and stick them in his desk, and then Eljam would come around and collect them. What was in those envelopes? Nadler told himself he didn't know, and he surely must have felt a sense of relief when they stopped being dropped off.

But then had come his deposition, for the Nakashes had apparently gotten wind of at least some of what was going on. And like a relentless, crushing python, the Nakash lawyer had wrapped himself around what facts he had and had begun to squeeze—incident after incident, envelope after envelope, visitor after visitor.

"Who gave you the envelope?" the lawyer had asked.

"An Oriental," Nadler had answered. *"It was a long time ago."*

"Do you know the man's name?" the lawyer had asked.

"I believe it was Hong," Nadler had answered. *"I believe it was Mr. Hong."*

"Is Mr. Hong a Guess contractor?"

"Yes."

"What company does he work for?"

"He runs a laundry service."

"What is the name of the laundry?"

"Homeway."

"Homewood?"

"Homeway."

"Is it true that Homeway laundry does stonewashing for Guess?"

"Yes."

"Do you recall when it was that Mr. Hong gave you this envelope?"

"I don't recall."
"Was it sometime during the summer of 1984?"
"I don't recall."
"Where were you when he gave you the envelope?"
"In my office."
"What size envelope was it?"
"I would say a standard size."
"Was it a regular letter-size envelope?"
"Letter size."

On and on the questions went. Was it a thick envelope or thin? What did Mr. Hong say when he gave it to you? Did you ever ask Mr. Hong what was in the envelope? How many times did this happen? What do you mean by "a few"? Who is Mr. Oh? Who is Mr. Chung? Who is Ms. Lee? Who is Peter Kwan? Do you recognize this document? Who prepared this invoice? Where do you live? What do you mean by "a lot"? Who else? When? Where? How many? Who else was present? When did you first learn this? Approximately how many times are we speaking of here? Was it more or less than ten? Who physically handed you the document? What was the substance of the telephone conversation? Did you take any notes? Was anyone else present?

It was exhausting, frightening. And no sooner was it over than the entire atmosphere around Guess began to change. Document shredders were suddenly everywhere. One day Nadler came to work and found armed guards patrolling the halls.

Finally, Nadler had gone to Maurice.

"I cannot live with this cloak-and-dagger routine," he'd said. He wanted out.

"Absolutely not," Maurice replied. "I will not accept that. I want the old Cary back."

Nadler liked to tell people he knew karate. He liked to portray himself as a fellow capable of handling situations as they developed. "I've had four years of it," he would say, "I can defend myself." But four years of karate hardly seemed enough for these circumstances. What good was karate when life seemed to consist of getting out of bed in the morning and spending the rest of the day wandering around inside a minefield?

Meanwhile, unfortunately, there was Armand's errand to attend to, and with the Peat Marwick accountant in tow, he headed off for the meeting. Bohbot's office wasn't far away, so the two men decided to walk. This was, after all, downtown Los Angeles in 1985, not some Moroccan Casbah.

Or was it? For scarcely had the two rounded a corner when suddenly out of nowhere a figure leaped from the shadows in a frenzy of flying hands and feet. Kicks and punches were landing everywhere, in Nadler's nose, his ribs.

How long it went on Nadler couldn't be sure. All he knew was that when it was over, the accountant lay sprawled on the pavement while Nadler watched with a broken nose as the man who had attacked them ran off down the street. It was berserk, insane. What was going on here?

Nadler tried to collect his thoughts. He was lucky to be alive. He bent down to help the accountant, and perhaps it was then that a wild and frightening thought dawned on him. He'd been in the fight of his life, but why hadn't the man tried to rob him? Maybe what had happened hadn't been a robbery attempt at all. Maybe . . . The possibilities seemed limitless. Were the Marcianos trying to warn him not to cooperate with the Nakashes? Maybe it was the Nakashes telling him to steer clear of the Marcianos. It was wheels within wheels until his mind reeled. And as he looked over to help the man from Peat Marwick, perhaps Nadler realized that for himself at least, nothing would be the same again ever—at least so long as he stayed at Guess.

Chapter 10

On the floor below Nadler's office worked Guess's chief financial officer, Bill Merrigan. Having joined Guess in January of 1985, Bill was still relatively new to the company. Yet he could hardly have avoided being struck by the strange tension of the place—particularly the conspiratorial vibes that seemed to flow from behind the closed doors of the boardroom pantry down the hall.

Every day for months now, the brothers had been arriving in Paul's limo first thing in the morning, then heading straight for the pantry. They'd go inside, close the door, and not come out all day. Everyone knew what was going on in there: They were plotting war against the Nakashes. But no one had any details. Often, the brothers wouldn't even break for lunch. Instead, a catering service would appear at around noon and they'd work right through. It was as if the company had been put on automatic pilot while its owners prepared to do battle with their enemies. Things were obviously going to be bloody too since, from beyond the barbed wire, the Nakashes were by now firing off deposition subpoenas like machine-gun bullets.

The paranoia of the place seemed almost thick enough to cut with a knife. Shredders had been installed everywhere—there were maybe ten scattered around the building by now—and they seemed to be in constant use, particularly in the boardroom pantry. Whenever Merrigan stuck his head in the door, some secretary—or maybe even Georges or Paul—seemed to be standing at the machine, feeding sheets of paper into it. "We don't want memos or paper around here," Merrigan later recalled Georges as telling him. "Don't put anything in writing."

What was the big secret? One day Merrigan recalled Georges made a joke of the whole thing. He told Merrigan, "Bill, how do you think I got my patterns and my markers? I went through other people's trash to get them. I don't want anybody to do that to me." But was Merrigan really expected to believe that? The great Georges Marciano a garbage thief?

Yet it seemed to frustrate Merrigan not to know what was really going on. After all, he was Guess's top financial officer as well as its top-ranked management employee (not counting, of course, the brothers themselves). Yet as far as being included in the brothers' inner councils, he might as well have been pushing a mop in maintenance and repair.

Merrigan had been in the company for less than a year, but he was already coming to the opinion that Guess could blow sky-high at any moment. Georges and Maurice had been at each other's throats from the minute Merrigan had walked through the door back in January. Now, Maurice wasn't even showing up for work anymore. Sometimes he would disappear for days at a time, and Paul and Georges would come to Merrigan and ask had he seen him, and Merrigan would just shake his head no.

The falling-out between Georges and Maurice was itself rather disturbing. Officially, Maurice's departure was described as a sabbatical. And so far as most people could tell, the fight that had precipitated it had involved a matter of real strategic concern to the company—which course would be best for Guess to follow in the future, to continue to preserve the exclusivity of its name and label, or to broaden out into licensing and mass market merchandising?

Yet Merrigan seemed to sense something deeper at work. And his suspicions simply intensified when, in the aftermath of Maurice's departure, he saw Georges storming around ripping up deals with subcontractors—a couple of which turned out to be companies in which Merrigan understood that Maurice himself had a stake.

As for Paul, well, what could one say? As far as Merrigan was concerned, Paul was a maniac. And Merrigan knew, because Merrigan saw the bills. It was Paul who hired the armed guards, Paul who had private eyes from Kroll spying on everyone. One time Paul even told Merrigan that it was he—Paul—who'd gotten the IRS after Jeff Bohbot. As far as Merrigan was concerned, Paul would stop at nothing, he was plainly psychotic.

This was not what Merrigan had expected when he joined Guess the previous January. What fool would have joined otherwise? As Merrigan understood things, he'd be coming into a thriving company with a bright future in the fashion industry—and with just this annoying little side dispute to get resolved in the meantime. Meanwhile, Merrigan would be assuming a position of real importance, with real responsibilities; he was going to be the second-in-command behind the brothers themselves.

Instead, it was obvious from day one that the only thing that mattered in the entire corporation was fighting the Nakashes—a task that had apparently been reserved exclusively for the Marcianos and their lawyers. Not only was there not much for him to do as Guess's chief financial officer, but the brothers had kept him busy in the meantime as the financial equivalent of their own personal au pair boy. He was spending up to 80 percent of his time handling their personal finances, things like arranging lines of credit for them and executing stock trades for their personal portfolios.

Nor did this appear to be a practice restricted to Merrigan alone. Take Georges's secretary, Jan. She also spent most of her time on Georges's personal business. She kept his books and records, followed up on stock trade orders. She even had a Quotron machine on her desk to monitor prices for him. Or take Jan's friend Muriel, who did the same sort of chores for Maurice. Between them, the two women were earning more than eighty-five thousand dollars a year from Guess, in return for which Georges had one of them running around looking for Ferraris he could buy, while Maurice had the other one checking on doctor's appointments and other such matters.

In fact, wherever he looked, it seemed to Merrigan that the Marcianos had fallen into the habit of treating Guess as a kind of personal piggy bank—as if the company's co-owners back in New York didn't exist. For instance, if one of the Marcianos needed some money, he wouldn't go to a bank, he'd go to Merrigan and get it from Guess. When one of the brothers needed some work done on his house—which was often—Guess maintenance personnel would be sent out to do it. When the brothers went on trips, everything they spent was billed to Guess, whether the trip was for business or pleasure. As far as Merrigan was concerned, Paul had the cushiest deal of all. As head of advertising for Guess, he'd set up a separate company—Art Design Agency—and as far as Merrigan could make out, was billing Guess for everything the agency spent—plus a 15 percent commission on top.

The brothers still owned their chain of trendy little jeanswear boutiques outright, since it hadn't been included in the deal with the

Nakashes, and Merrigan spent a great deal of time helping out there as well. He hired accountants, oversaw the installation of a computer system, negotiated a line of credit. He was doing all these things for the Marcianos personally, but he wasn't doing much of anything for the company that was paying his hundred-thousand-dollar-a-year salary—Guess.

Merrigan had known the Marcianos through Mitsui-Manufacturers Bank, where he had worked as a loan officer. Merrigan's branch had a number of garment industry clients, and the Marcianos were among them. Their accounts were handled by Merrigan himself, which was how he'd gotten to know the brothers in the first place. He processed loan applications for them, took care of deposit accounts, credit references, and other such matters. One day, according to Merrigan, Maurice mentioned to him that he wanted to set up some separate accounts under the names of some new firms that Merrigan had never heard of before. Merrigan didn't seem to pay too much attention to the subject at the time, but now that he'd gone to work for the brothers it was possible to see that maybe he should have: Some of the names on those accounts were the same as the ones that the Nakashes were now saying were part of the Marciano kickback scheme.

In fact, it seemed like only weeks after he'd joined the company when the shredders had begun appearing and people had started whispering about the kickback thing. Nadler's deposition in April had certainly gotten the ball rolling, but the brothers had obviously known something was up even before then. Merrigan recalled being in Maurice's office a week or so before the Nadler deposition while Maurice dictated a memo to the Nakashes on this very subject; suddenly Maurice had turned to Georges, who was also in the room, and joked, "Can you believe they found out about it?"

Merrigan would have been the first to admit that in the world of high finance, he was no Wall Street rocket scientist. He had attended the University of Louisville but had failed to earn a degree. He was, in fact, in many respects just a red-blooded American Joe. A single man in his thirties in Los Angeles, he had a healthy eye for the ladies, he enjoyed a good Friday night game of cards with pals from the old days back at the bank, and he liked to toss back a few with the boys after hours when the occasion arose. But Merrigan's eyes worked as well as the next guy's, and from nine to five he saw what he saw. The tension was enormous, as the brothers would scream and shout constantly at subordinates and even at one another over seemingly inconsequential concerns. This obviously wasn't a healthy situation he'd managed to wander into, but when it came time to depart would it be so easy to wander back out?

Chapter 11

On a nippy afternoon that December, a visitor called on Avi Nakash in his office above the garment district. It was Hardof Wolf, the Israeli businessman who had promoted the original Nakash investment in Guess more than two years earlier. Some people seem to fall asleep dreaming schemes, and Hardof was such a person. He wasn't exactly Iago, but he wasn't Ward Cleaver either. It was because of Wolf that the Marcianos and Nakashes had come together in the first place, and look at what had resulted.

Now, with the Marcianos and Nakashes at each other's throats, and lawsuits popping up left and right, Wolf thought he saw an opportunity to make yet another commission off this ill-fated union—by brokering its breakup.

Though he spoke with a heavy Hebrew accent, Wolf bore a strong resemblance to the American folk-rock singer John Denver. From his wide smile and angular features, to his full head of reddish brown hair and a preference for wire-rimmed glasses, Wolf looked younger than his forty-eight years. Yet he was also a veteran of many years' experience in both the garment industry and Middle Eastern business, and he was a lawyer to boot. Beneath the disarming exterior lurked a man who had survived a lifetime of swimming in some of the most shark-infested waters on earth.

In fact, though he had come claiming a desire to help Avi resolve his differences with the Marcianos, Wolf actually seemed to be working both sides of the street, and was simultaneously pursuing a secret mission that Avi would hardly have approved of at all. Its goal: to convince a former Jordache warehouse manager to testify against the Nakashes at the trial. Wolf was some operator.

Yet so was Avi. And unfortunately for Wolf, the individual he was seeking to enlist against the Nakashes was the worst person possible. By the labyrinthine connections of Middle Eastern Sephardim, the person in question turned out to be related by marriage to the Na- kashes themselves. As luck would have it, the person Wolf had targeted —Shlomo Shaul by name—happened to be the cousin of Ralph Na- kash's wife, Rosanne. As a result, Wolf had scarcely begun making overtures before word of his maneuvers got back to the brothers. In Israel they say, Your friend has a friend, and your friend's friend has a friend, so be discreet.

Although Wolf didn't realize it, thanks to his gamesmanship, Avi no longer seemed to trust Wolf much at all, and in fact would soon begin maneuvering to turn Wolf's double-dealing against him—if he hadn't done so already. In those shark-infested waters, it looked as if Wolf had swum upon one of the biggest sharks of all.

Avi's scheme was simple yet clever—a perhaps unwitting update on one of Judaism's oldest stories. In Hebrew tradition, the archangel Gabriel is constantly recording the deeds of men on the scrolls of the heavenly host, to be argued over at the last atonement by the forces of darkness and light. But when Shaul told Avi that Wolf had turned up at Shaul's Los Angeles warehouse soliciting backstabbing testimony against the Nakashes, it didn't take the Nakash brother long to figure an improvement on scrolls. Why rely on written words when he could have the sins of the betrayer straight from his own lips? In Aleppo they say, A donkey is tied by his reins, a person by his tongue. And Avi figured to tie a great big knot around the tongue of Hardof Wolf.

The plan: Shaul was to go out and buy a pocket tape recorder and secretly tape everything Wolf said if he ever came back—and, of course, give the tape to Avi as soon as Wolf left.

A few days later Wolf did call back, and Shaul was ready. Moistening the little rubber suction cup that fit on the receiver, he switched on the machine and secretly began recording the conversation. At the end of the week, Wolf called back again, and Shaul repeated the ritual.

Then he telephoned Avi in New York, and played the tape—directly into *Avi's* own secret recorder. What the Nakash brother heard no doubt made his blood boil, for here was a man claiming to be a media- tor in a deal—secretly working for Avi's worst enemy.

Meanwhile, Wolf was now seated in Avi's very office, oblivious to the fact that his string with the Nakashes was already beginning to run out.

"Avi," said Wolf, "we talk level, okay?"

"Sure," agreed Nakash, "we talk level." And the conversation began.

What exactly Wolf did for a living was hard to say. He claimed to be self-employed and would variously describe himself as being in everything from real estate to "business investments." He maintained a home in Tel Aviv and another in Beverly Hills, and claimed dual residencies in Israel and the United States. He also seemed to live in constant fear of his tax status with the IRS, and once, when asked during a deposition where he maintained his offices, he answered that he worked out of the back seat of his car.

Wolf's involvement with the Marcianos went back years. Though he often claimed vaguely to have met Georges on a bench one day in Los Angeles at around the time he began brokering an investment in Guess, he had in fact been a partner with the Marcianos years earlier when he acquired a one-half interest in one of their first boutiques. Thereafter, Wolf had learned that the brothers were in need of money and were eager to sell their jeans manufacturing business, so he began quietly looking around for a buyer.

Wolf put out feelers to upwards of ten different people whom he thought might be interested in an up-and-coming young California jeans maker. At one point a potential buyer suggested he might be interested in half the company for $1 million. But it seemed a ridiculously low bid, especially since the Marcianos had already told him they'd sell the whole company for $10 million. In the end, all turned him down anyway. Was there something about the deal that was frightening people off?

Eventually, Wolf brought up the subject with an Israeli named Yosi Gilboa, a friend who had been introduced to him by a man in the diamond business, and who happened to have business ties to the Nakashes. Wolf was hoping Gilboa knew of somebody who might be interested in the investment, and if that somebody turned out to be the Nakashes, so much the better.

Gilboa was hardly the sort of person most people would want to claim as a friend. In fact, with Gilboa, betrayal reached heights that would have caused even the assassins of ancient Persia to swoon. In 1970 he'd participated in an armed robbery in Switzerland. Then, to lighten his sentence, he'd struck a deal with the Swiss police, who'd wanted him to finger his accomplices. Gilboa didn't want to name the pal who'd committed the robbery with him, so he thought and thought. Whom could he blame instead?

At last Gilboa remembered a man named Ben, whom he'd met once in Los Angeles. Ben had nothing to do with robbery. In fact, Ben had nothing to do with Gilboa either; Gilboa had simply said hello to him once in Los Angeles. So to curry favor with the Swiss police, Gilboa told them that Ben had been part of the robbery. Now, Gilboa was was walking around free, while Ben was hiding out in Israel, the only country in the world from which Switzerland couldn't extradite him—for a crime he never committed.

Yet friend or backstabber, Gilboa was also involved with the Nakashes, and Wolf knew that it was pointless to hold his past against him. In the garment industry, people who got too picky could wind up with no friends at all.

Though Wolf and Gilboa wound up having several talks about whether the Nakashes might be interested in buying Guess, the idea got a blunt turndown when Gilboa pitched it to Joe Nakash, the head of the family.

"There's a company in L.A. called Guess that's doing about $6 million in business and it's got a lot of name recognition out here," said Gilboa. "Are you interested?"

"We're very busy, and I just don't have time for another small company," Joe replied.

Gilboa tried again several weeks later, but when Joe persisted he backed off and let the matter drop.

Later, when Wolf was questioned under oath about the matter, he said the turndown had left him "quite disappointed," and it's not hard to see why: Whether or not the investment would have been good for the Nakashes and the Marcianos, it clearly would have been good for both Gilboa and Wolf, who stood to collect brokerage fees if a deal went through. As the middleman who had initiated the transaction, Wolf alone could have collected perhaps as much as $150,000 as his share of the deal's 3 percent commission fee.

So both men put their heads together. Wasn't there a way the two sides could be nudged together?

At last Gilboa came up with an idea: Since Joe wasn't interested in investing in Guess, why not try Avi? A week or so later he gave the youngest Nakash a call. Next thing Joe Nakash knew, Avi was standing in his office doorway, suggesting that they take a second look at the Guess deal.

But Joe told him he wasn't interested.

"We don't need it," he said. "Why bother?" After all, what was a measly little $6 million-a-year business for a company that was already enjoying gross revenues of $240 million annually?

But Avi wasn't to be discouraged and called Gilboa back and said they were interested.

So Gilboa called Wolf. "I think there is a possibility that Jordache will buy shares in Guess," he announced. "We should proceed in this direction."

Wolf immediately telephoned the Marcianos to tell them that he might have a buyer. Further conversations followed, and finally, when it looked like he had the Marcianos' terms nailed down, he looped around Gilboa and called Avi Nakash with an offer: Georges was willing to part with the whole company—all the shares—for ten million dollars.

"I'm not negotiating," he hastened to add, as Avi listened, "just transferring."

Avi sounded positive about the offer, so as soon as he hung up, Wolf telephoned the Marcianos again. By now he was so excited that he lost track of who he was speaking to, whether Maurice or Georges.

"I have a potential buyer for ten million dollars," he declared.

Thereafter, so many telephone calls took place with so many people that Wolf lost track altogether. There were calls to Gilboa, more calls with Avi and the Marcianos, and finally a meeting was set up for that weekend at Wolf's home in Beverly Hills.

A delegation of Jordache officials boarded a plane for L.A., and when the group returned a day or so later, everyone gathered in Joe's office.

"They're nice people," said Avi. "They have lots of orders, and there's name recognition too. I've got a good feeling about this."

A week or so later there was a second meeting, this one in Georges's apartment. After that came a third meeting, then a fourth and a fifth. Before long, Wolf was no longer attending the meetings at all as the lawyers and accountants took over. But Wolf didn't seem to care, and in a sense, why should he? After all, he'd brought the parties together, and one way or another he was going to get his money.

Now, two years later here he sat, hoping to help Avi Nakash climb back out of the hole he'd helped dig for him in the first place. Once again, it all came down to money, and once again, it was Wolf trying to nail down a price.

Avi didn't seem impressed, so the conversation dragged on, and finally Wolf left. Yet if anyone had told him, as he left Avi's office, that three and a half years later he'd be standing before a federal grand jury that wanted to know—incredibly enough—whether what had happened that day in Avi's office was part of a Marciano extortion plot, Wolf no doubt would have been amazed. On the other hand, maybe he shouldn't have been, for when it came to the Marcianos and the Nakashes, no one needed to spell out for Hardof Wolf how little things could grow into huge concerns for everyone. In fact, it wouldn't take long before Wolf would begin to see such a mountain growing before his eyes.

Chapter 12

It was shortly before 8:00 A.M. on January 28, 1986, when a caravan of cars bearing U.S. government license plates began coiling through midtown Manhattan toward the garment district. It had snowed the night before, and the morning was blustery and wet, with slush in the gutters and ice on the sidewalks.

Along Broadway the workday had already begun, and the young black men who pushed the pipe racks back and forth through the streets cinched their sweatshirt hoods more tightly than ever about their heads and leaned into their tasks. In the cold, people seemed to move a little faster, be a little more self-absorbed. It was the sort of day when someone could pull a pistol in the Chock Full O'Nuts and empty out the cash register, and no one would notice.

In the caravan's lead car sat a short, rumpled man in a raincoat. In his hand he held a sketch of a floor plan, and from time to time he would glance down at it. It was the floor plan of Jordache Enterprises' fifth-floor offices. It had been prepared on the basis of information provided by Paul Marciano, and the man holding it was Steve Levy, the same IRS criminal investigator who had briefly surfaced in the case six months earlier when he had flown to Los Angeles to meet with Saranow and review the Kroll material on the Nakashes.

Saranow and Levy had met a second time in New York, and Levy had seemed a bit in awe of the West Coast official, with his tennis-court tan and his trim California physique. Over dinner the two had slipped into small talk that wound up seeming to make Levy feel even worse. Saranow had talked of his exploits as a jogger, of his skill in mixed doubles. Not to be outclassed totally, Levy had volunteered some information regarding his own athletic exploits.

"I've run the New York marathon twice," he declared.

"Really?" asked Saranow. "How did you do?"

"That was just it," Levy confessed. "Mostly I had to walk. But I finished!" Then, as if to end on a positive note, he added, "I always finish what I start."

Now, Levy was about to engage in another kind of contest in which speed alone was not enough—an IRS tax raid. Nearly a half-year after they'd first approached Howard Wilson charging criminal tax evasion by the Nakashes, the Marcianos were at last to get what they'd been seeking. The men in the caravan, close to fifty in all, were special agents of the Internal Revenue Service and the U.S. Customs Service, and they had come bearing a subpoena, which Levy held in his pocket. The document had been signed by U.S. Attorney Rudolph Giuliani, authorizing the group to enter Jordache's offices, by force if necessary, and seize the firm's books and records—all of them.

As the caravan swung to curbside, Levy knew what had to be done. It was important to hit the offices with swiftness and surprise, otherwise the paperwork they were looking for could be moving through shredders before they got off the elevators. But they also had to be thorough—as thorough and careful as Levy had ever before been in his career. In the words of the search warrant in his pocket, he was to "seize and prepare a written inventory" of virtually every piece of paper to be found on the Jordache premises.

After listening to what Paul had to say to the grand jury, the U.S. Attorney's Office wanted everything. If their so-called Witness X knew what he was talking about (and he obviously did), Jordache must have been an anthill of tax fraud and crime, and the feds were going to kick the place apart. They were going to turn on the IRS vacuum cleaner and suck Jordache dry—and in the end they were going to say, "Thank you very much, ma'am—just doing our jobs," like a squad of Joe Fridays in *Dragnet*.

They wanted all bookkeeping and accounting records, all evidence of receipts and disbursements, all ledgers and pay books, all cash receipt books, all payroll ledgers and time cards. They wanted all sales journals, all purchase journals, all financial statements (certified, qualified, or otherwise), all accountants' work papers, all documents pertaining to tax filings.

They wanted all bank statements, canceled checks, deposit or withdrawal tickets, letters of credit, loan agreements, notes, mortgages, incorporation papers, shareholder lists, minutes of board meetings, intercompany contracts and agreements, correspondence, and letters.

They wanted all import and export documents, cost lists, purchase orders, quota transfer records, invoices, debit notes and memos, bills of lading, carrier records, packing lists and slips, export licenses, consumption entry forms, trademark registrations.

Not only did they want the originals of all those documents, they also wanted all archival, computerized, microfilm or microfiche backup for them. Commanded by the search warrant in his pocket, Levy and his group were to enter the offices of the largest privately owned jeans company in America and walk out with the complete documentary record of every transaction ever undertaken in its name by any of its employees, officers, or owners from January 1, 1981, to the present. Levy was surely glad they were acting on solid information—that the Marcianos and Kroll had built a good case—otherwise, this operation could wind up looking like the biggest fishing expedition of all time.

The building's lobby was cramped, and as the agents crowded in, they filled it to overflowing, forcing secretaries and other office workers to stand outside and mill about on the sidewalk. For trip after trip the building's elevator hauled the men to the fifth floor, where Levy reassembled them, then marched down the hall in the direction of the Jordache offices. Many of the agents carried guns, several carried crowbars and sledgehammers to smash down doors and pry open files.

The main entrance was open, and a number of Jordache's employees were already at work when the agents burst in and Levy bellowed, "Freeze! Move away from your desks! Move!"

Startled employees looked up. Before them was a scowling mob of armed men streaming out through the office in all directions, rifling through desks, tagging file cabinets for removal. At a loss for what else to do, Avi's secretary, a young Brooklynite named Susan, began trailing along behind some of the men, trying to keep a tally of what they were scooping up and hauling off. But it was hopeless. Too much was going on everywhere to keep track of anything.

The seizure order required the federal agents to vacate the Jordache premises by the end of the day. But it soon became clear that the agents would never be through by quitting time. There was just too much to catalog and cart off: invoices, checks, order forms, patterns, minutes of meetings, memoranda—the list ran on endlessly. They were like the people in *Willy Wonka and the Chocolate Factory,* opening every candy bar in the place just to find the one golden ticket inside. In the desk of Jordache's in-house counsel, a slicked-back lawyer named Robert Spiegelman, the agents found fifteen audio cassette tapes, collections of interoffice memos, and numerous sets of record books and file folders; and a nearby credenza was stuffed with yet more folders. And this was just in one office, in a fifth-floor rabbit warren of more than fifty such cubicles.

So on the work went: desk after desk, cabinet after cabinet, room after room. Personnel, accounting, production, marketing; out the door and down the elevator went the documents—by the hundreds, by the thousands. It was like opening a closet door and discovering the Brooklyn Public Library inside. This wasn't just any old document seizure, this was turning into one of the biggest paper-grabs in the history of the IRS.

By mid-afternoon it was clear to Levy that he'd need another day or the agents would never finish, and he telephoned the U.S. Attorney's Office to ask if the vacate-time could be extended for twenty-four hours. An hour or so later back came permission, courtesy of a federal magistrate, and the tagging and loading continued.

Three thousand miles away in Beverly Hills, Paul Marciano woke early and went downstairs for a breakfast of coffee and croissants. A voracious reader, Paul would normally consume *The New York Times,* the *Los Angeles Times, The Wall Street Journal,* and *Women's Wear Daily* before leaving the table. Thanks to the fight with the Nakashes, he now paid particular attention to stories involving lawsuits and white-collar crime, and had lately been following with interest the tidbits that had begun to trickle out regarding political corruption in the administration of New York's Mayor Edward Koch. As Paul sized the situation up, U.S. Attorney Giuliani had probably already opened a probe of his own—or soon would—and he wondered what, if anything, this might do to slow Giuliani's investigation of the Nakashes.

On this day the big story in the *Times* was the scheduled launching that morning of the Challenger space shuttle, a subject that bored Paul to tears. The front page of *The Wall Street Journal* would have proved more interesting, especially a left-hand column feature piece that Paul had no doubt been hoping to see—especially considering the slowpoke pace at which things had been proceeding in Giuliani's office. For weeks Paul had been asking himself what the holdup was, yet now splayed across the front page of *The Wall Street Journal* was as good a reason to act as they'd need.

The article, entitled "Smuggler's Heaven," dealt with the "$40 billion in contraband and counterfeit goods" that slip past U.S. Customs inspectors each year. Smuggled goods were said to range from Cabbage Patch dolls to steel pipe and clothing.

Finally, toward the bottom of the page, there it was—not simply a mere mention but five whole paragraphs.

Alleged irregularities of a different sort have surfaced in a lawsuit involving Jordache Enterprises, one of the largest designer-apparel companies in the U.S. A Hong Kong affiliate of Jordache, Jordache International, has been accused of . . .

For weeks the Kroll people had been saying that action was imminent. But when, when? That was what Paul wanted to know. Now even *The Wall Street Journal* had picked up the story. It was smuggler's paradise out there, yet here was half the country going nuts over New York City corruption and the other half barely able to restrain itself over a Space Shuttle launch. Had the world gone mad? The Nakashim were on the loose and it said so right there on the front page of *The Wall Street Journal*.

Paul was just rising from the table when the telephone rang. The call was from New York, and on the other end was a breathless and panting friend wanting to know if Paul had heard the news: The Jordache building across the street had just been raided by federal agents. The power had apparently been cut off, and the employees had all been sent home; armed agents were said to be everywhere.

It took a moment for the import to sink in. A raid? The Nakashes? Then it dawned on him. This was what he'd been waiting for! The raid! The raid! The Nakashes were being raided!

"It'll be on TV," Paul cried. "Call me back later," and he ran across the room and flipped on a set.

Yet maddeningly enough, there was no raid news at all. Wherever he flipped the dial, every channel had the same thing—the damned space shuttle. It was poised on its launch pad, with clouds of steam billowing out all around. Then came the disembodied voice of Mission Control: ten, nine, eight, seven, six . . .

Jesus Christ, Paul later recalled thinking, the New York garment district was erupting in flames, and all the media could cover was another fucking space trip! Didn't the damned press know a story when it was staring them in the face? Impulsively he snapped off the set and reached for the phone, thinking, Grossman, Grossman! I've got to find my lawyer. It was thrilling. At last the Nakashes were going to get theirs!

Chapter 13

As luck would have it, Ralph and Joe Nakash were in Los Angeles on the morning of the raid, and this left Avi to deal with the crisis alone. It was an appalling situation, yet in a way perfectly fitting, for as Avi no doubt thought more than once that day, if it hadn't been for him there wouldn't have been a raid in the first place. If he'd only listened to his older brothers instead of his own "good feeling," the Nakashes wouldn't now be 50 percent owners of a cesspool, and federal agents wouldn't be crawling through Jordache's offices, hauling out files by the truckload.

In the folk wisdom of the Middle East it is said that there is one irredeemable sin—the singular misfortune from which no one may recover—and that is the humiliation that comes from the loss of face. And look at the face that Avi had lost! In the old country there was an expression: Roast pigeons don't fly into an open mouth. For a time, perhaps Avi had thought otherwise. He'd spied his pigeon and opened his mouth hungrily—and in had flown four bloodsucking vultures!

By the end of the day more than 450 crates had been hauled out on dollies. Out of Spiegelman's office alone came thirty cartons. About the only files the company by now had left were whatever existed in Hong Kong, which mainly consisted of the books and records of Jordache International and its associated companies. How could Jordache now pay its bills? How could it reconstruct who owed it what? How would it meet its payroll? Who in fact was *on* the payroll?

The Hong Kong files were at least one place to start looking for some answers, so after much frantic back-and-forth telephoning between New York and Los Angeles, Joe and Ralph boarded a flight to Hong Kong to try to assess the damage. Avi would stay in New York and do whatever was possible from there.

In fact, neither Ralph nor Joe knew that Paul Marciano had begun monitoring their movements. Like a hundred-eyed Argos, he had deployed spies and informants everywhere, and was getting reports from both coasts. As soon as he learned that the two Nakash brothers had boarded a Hong Kong–bound flight from Los Angeles International Airport, he concluded that this *proved* they were guilty. Guilty of exactly what, he wasn't yet sure, but they were certainly guilty of something! After all, with their company in New York being pillaged by the feds, why else would they be flying eight thousand miles in the opposite direction? To Paul there seemed but one answer: to clean out their files of all incriminating documents!

But no Nakash was going to get the jump on a Marciano. In their trip to Hong Kong back before Christmas, Paul and Marshall Grossman had already lined up a local solicitor to represent them, and the man was now well along in preparing papers for a so-called Anton Pillar order. Such a writ is unknown in the United States, but in Crown Colony law it allows private civil litigants to swear out court orders authorizing the police to enter private offices and seize documents and records if a danger exists that the documents might otherwise be destroyed or falsified. And if there was one thing Paul Marciano was certain of, it was that the Nakashes were capable of falsifying or destroying anything.

Not, however, if Paul got there first! Initially, Paul had figured it would take the Hong Kong solicitor eight to ten weeks to prepare the paperwork for the seizure order. But now had come the raid in New York, and suddenly everything was happening at lightning speed, climaxing, it seemed, in the spectacle of Ralph and Joe jetting off to Asia to destroy all the evidence of their crimes.

Earlier in the day Paul had tracked down Marshall Grossman in New York, where the Marciano lawyer was taking a deposition in a separate case on behalf of the firm of Wachtell, Lipton, Rosen & Katz. Unfortunately, when he called the Wachtell, Lipton number in New York, he was told that Grossman had already left for Kennedy Airport and was about to board a flight back to Los Angeles.

Paul was at his wits' end. Was Grossman even aware of what was going on? Here he was, Paul Marciano, the brains behind the raid, stuck in Los Angeles with his lawyer out of touch in a plane somewhere over America while the loathsome Nakashes were heading off to Hong Kong to cover their tracks!

It was late that afternoon when Grossman's flight finally touched down at Los Angeles International Airport. Grossman was tired from the flight, and was grateful that his office had arranged for a limousine to pick him up for the ride home. Yet scarcely had the car left Century Boulevard and turned north onto the freeway than the cellular telephone rang. On the other end was Paul Marciano.

"We've got to go to Hong Kong immediately!" Paul cried. "Tonight! We've got to get there before Ralph and Joe! There's no time to lose!"

Grossman had no idea what the man was talking about. Hong Kong? No time to lose? Had something happened that he hadn't heard about?

"You don't understand," Paul continued. "It's because of the raid. Ralph and Joe are already on their way to Hong Kong. They're going to destroy evidence. We've got to leave right now. Armand's coming."

Wait a minute, said Grossman. He wanted Paul to slow down—at least let him call home first.

The following minutes were an eternity for Paul. He didn't want to be waiting for phone calls at a time like this. He wanted action! Results! Get up and go!

Moments later the phone rang and it was Grossman from the limo.

"Three seats," he said, "first thing in the morning."

For Avi Nakash, meanwhile, events likewise must have been passing in a blur. Inspired partly by a need to do *something,* lawyers were brought in to take statements from employees about how they'd been treated, and by week's end the glimmerings of a routine had begun to return to his life. But it didn't last long, for just after supper on Saturday evening the telephone rang with yet more astounding news: Jordache's offices in Hong Kong were being raided. The police were everywhere and the company's books and records had been impounded. It was a replay of what had happened in New York only ninety-six hours earlier.

What Avi said or felt at the time isn't known. Yet years later, he recalled that week as having been one of the ghastliest moments of his life, and small wonder. On Tuesday, Jordache's offices in New York had been raided by the IRS. Now it was Saturday night and the Hong Kong police were doing the same thing to his operation on the other side of the earth. This was impossible. Suddenly it seemed that half the law enforcement agencies in the English-speaking world were after him. But for what? What? These accursed Marcianos were destroying his life!

Chapter 14

Though the raid had been as disruptive to the Nakashes as anything the Marcianos might have hoped for, scarcely had the seized documents been hauled off before, oddly enough, interest in the case began to wane—at least inside the office of U.S. Attorney Rudolph Giuliani.

It wasn't as if the case had suddenly become unimportant, it was rather that other, even bigger cases began pouring in from everywhere. The Colombo crime family and Pizza Connection cases had already breathed new life into the Organized Crime Unit on the ninth floor, which had withered under Giuliani's predecessor, John Martin. Now an investigation was under way against mobster Anthony "Fat Tony" Salerno as well, and the list of targets seemed to grow longer by the day.

Meanwhile, down the hall from Giuliani's office on the eighth floor, cases had begun to multiply in the long-dormant Public Corruption Unit. In October, embezzlement had been uncovered in New York City's Human Resources Administration. In January, a grand jury had been impaneled to investigate corruption in the city's Parking Violations Bureau, and by March, Bronx Democratic party boss Stanley Friedman had been indicted on racketeering and conspiracy charges. That same month an investigation was opened into Pentagon-related corruption charges involving Bronx-based Wedtech Corporation, the largest defense contractor in the city.

Down on the sixth floor, potentially the biggest investigation of all was brewing. From out of the blue, a tip had come to the Securities and Exchange Commission regarding insider trading by a Drexel Burnham Lambert investment banker named Dennis Levine. By now, prosecutors and SEC investigators were secretly tussling for control of the case, as more and more revelations poured from Levine's lips every day.

"I can't even begin to describe what it was like," said Robert Plotz, an assistant prosecutor in the Securities Fraud Unit. "There just wasn't enough time to do half of what had to be done—yet every day it seemed we had to do more."

Howard Wilson, the chief of the Criminal Division at the time, looked back years later and agreed. "I think I just had too much to do. It was a problem for everyone."

Somehow, news of the turmoil didn't quite seem to reach through to the floor above. Or if it did, it was apparently either ignored or discounted, as each passing day brought yet more Giuliani press conferences announcing even bigger indictments and cases. An adulatory cover story in *The New York Times* Sunday magazine had already reported the boss's penchant for measuring performance by the number of indictments rather than by ultimate convictions and had gone on to portray him as a virtual one-man bulwark against crime and corruption. The article quoted him as saying, "My view is: The way you end corruption, you scare the daylights out of people." Since then, Giuliani had held eleven more press conferences on various Southern District investigations—eclipsing the media exposure of even U.S. Attorney General Edwin Meese.

As for the Jordache tax case, never seemingly very interesting to Giuliani to begin with, it now apparently dropped off his radar screen altogether. One reason may simply have been the difficulty Lorna Schofield seemed to be having giving the sheer immensity of the case a focus. To those around her, it was as if the IRS raid had grabbed so much paper that Schofield had begun to lose her bearings—as if the evidence she now possessed created as much confusion as clarification.

Giuliani seemed to sense it as well, particularly when the Major Crimes Unit assembled in his office once a month to update him on individual cases. When the talk got around to the Jordache tax investigation, Schofield would reportedly seem to have trouble explaining what was actually going on. Who could follow the twisting, convoluted case anyway, with its soundalike brothers and their backstabbing intrigues?

"She just never got control of the case," recalled a onetime colleague, Ken Schacter, who went on to join a law firm representing Guess in the fight. "The investigation just grew too enormous and sprawling. It ran away with her."

Unfortunately for Schofield, the ever-extending tentacles of the Southern District were now about to entangle her in something bigger and more baffling than even the Jordache case. Dealing with the Nakashes and Marcianos was bad enough. But though she would never have guessed it, she was about to be dragged into what would soon become known as the Iran-contra scandal.

The origins of the case traced back to the previous December, when a slippery Iranian banker named Cyrus Hashemi approached the government with a deal. Hashemi had gotten himself in trouble in an arms case a couple of years earlier, and to avoid trial on the rap, he now wanted to trade some information. Specifically, Hashemi claimed he had evidence of a plot to smuggle arms to Iran and was willing to trade that information in return for getting his own earlier indictment dropped. The alleged plot involved a partner in a white-shoe New York law firm, a Hollywood character actor, and even Adnan Kashoggi, the reputed Saudi Arabian billionaire.

Unfortunately, what Hashemi didn't reveal was that all involved—himself included—had initially become mixed up in the deal in the belief that the arms shipments in question were being covertly supported by the Reagan administration, which had indicated its willingness to look the other way as arrangements progressed.

Intrigued by his half-told story, the prosecutors decided to turn Hashemi into a government informant, wiring him up with a hidden tape recorder and sending him back out to consummate his deal. Months of skulduggery followed, then in April 1986, fifteen of the alleged conspirators were arrested—some nabbed in New York, while others were rounded up as they stepped off a plane in Bermuda. A day after that, Giuliani was standing before press conference cameras to announce the breakup of what was said to be an international smuggling ring preparing to ship more than $2 billion worth of military gear illegally to Teheran.

A day later, Lorna Schofield was handed the case—another snake pit of scheming, hissing Old World businessmen.

Aside from what Giuliani had said at his press conference, Schofield knew next to nothing of the background to the case—any more than she knew of the bottomless intrigues in the Jordache matter. Neither, for that matter, did her new boss as head of Major Crimes, a redheaded young man named Stuart Abrams. In the frenzied world of the Southern District, even unit chiefs who had been around for years didn't know much about the caseloads of their assistants. No formal reporting system existed to keep track of anything, and many assistants weren't even sure themselves how many cases they had.

All Schofield knew was that scarcely had she been handed the case than problems began to erupt from it like acne. Not only did many of the defendants turn out to be apparently respectable people, but they all had lots of money and promptly hired dozens of the best, most troublesome criminal defense lawyers in the country. Lead counsel for them all was the firm of Grand & Ostrow—as luck would have it, the same firm that was representing Jordache.

"It was impossible," Schofield said later. "Whenever I had something to do on one case, they'd swamp me with pleadings and motions on the other case. It was like I just gave up sleeping."

Worst of all, hardly were arraignments over when defense lawyers began proclaiming the whole case absurd because Washington had authorized everything in advance.

"How could these people possibly get jet fighters without government involvement somewhere?" cried William Kunstler, the same courtroom grandstander who'd made her life hell in the Black Liberation Army case.

Yet whenever she turned to superiors for help, no one seemed to have the time even to think about the matter, let alone suggest how to handle it. "Defendants always say things like that," they'd tell her, "just forget about it and go forward."

Sometimes in quiet moments Schofield would sit at her desk and mull over what to do. But in the end there really seemed no choice. The entire office was as overworked as she was, so how could she say she couldn't handle both cases? Under the circumstances, the Jordache case would simply have to take care of itself for a while. After all, how many headaches could one young assistant prosecutor handle at a time?

Chapter 15

About twenty miles from the Marciano homes in Beverly Hills, in the garment district of downtown Los Angeles, a telephone rang in the factory office of Shlomo Shaul—the cousin of Ralph Nakash's wife, Rosie.

It had been weeks since Shaul had secretly tape-recorded Hardof Wolf's conversation and passed it on to Avi. Yet now that the IRS had raided Jordache's offices in New York, Shaul had reason to worry about what he had done. Suppose the tape had been seized by the government. So far as he knew, what he had done had been legal, but it sure didn't look very good, and suppose news of it somehow got out. The raid itself was the talk of the garment industry, and if Shaul wasn't careful he might wind up dragged into it—through no fault of his own.

At thirty-two, Shaul was having trouble getting going in his career. He had come to the United States from Israel at the start of the 1980s, and because his cousin Rosie was Ralph Nakash's wife, he'd landed a job with Jordache as a warehouse manager in Los Angeles. But things hadn't worked out. Ralph hadn't been pleased with how he'd handled the job, and when Shaul's father fell ill in Israel and Shaul flew home to be with him, Ralph brought in a replacement as warehouse manager. Then when Shaul returned from Israel, he found the new man apparently in the job for good.

"You lost control of the warehouse," Ralph told him vaguely by way of explanation. "I think it's better for both of us if you find another job."

Shaul left and decided to start his own company, just as the Nakashes had done. He called it D'Champs and it lasted two weeks. Once again, things just weren't working out.

One thing led to another, and Shaul eventually found himself owner of a garment dye shop, one of the many such small-scale subcontracting operations in the jeans industry. His company was called Apha Dye House, and Shaul had tried to move it into the big time, but it was difficult. He'd tried to land an account with Guess, but failed. Currently, his main customer was Jordache—as if his venture into free enterprise capitalism had literally turned him in a circle.

Now, the ringing telephone was about to bring the most head-spinning—and disturbing—development yet in his relations with the two groups of brothers.

On the other end was a woman.

Hello, she said, Shlomo?

Yes, Shaul answered, who's there?

It was Muriel—Maurice Marciano's secretary. It seemed that Maurice wanted to know if Shlomo would be in his office for the next twenty minutes. Something had apparently come up.

Shaul agreed; he would be there. But before he could ask what was going on, Muriel had hung up.

Not long afterward came a knock at the door. What could Maurice want of him?

Come in, he said, and the door swung open.

But it wasn't Maurice Marciano at all. Standing before him instead were two strangers.

They wanted to talk to him about Nakash, said one.

About Jordache, added the other.

"Who are you?" asked Shaul. "What you want?"

"We are IRS special agents," said the short rumpled one. "We want to ask you questions about Nakash and Jordache."

What were they doing there? Why did they want to talk to him?

"Did Maurice Marciano sent you?" said Shaul.

We ask the questions, not you, said the short one. You used to work for Jordache didn't you?

"What your name?" asked Shaul. What was this all about?

Levy, answered the short one. The other man just pulled out a business card and handed it over.

What followed thereafter was for Shaul all a blur. The Nakashes took cash, didn't they? the two kept saying. If you don't say so you're a liar! Tell us or we'll destroy your business. Tell us what you know! You were the warehouse manager, weren't you? You knew all about what they did! Tell us the truth. Don't be a liar!

"Get out, get out!" cried Shaul at last. "I got nothing to say."

The two stared at him menacingly for some moments, then, as abruptly as they had arrived, they turned around and left.

No sooner had they left than Shaul had Avi on the phone in New York,

"Avi," he said, "what just happened . . . !" And he began to relay the news: that Maurice Marciano had called and told him to stay in his office, and then two guys from the IRS had shown up, and they tried to make him say things that weren't true—some guy Levy from New York and somebody from local—and they wanted to know why he was protecting criminals. What was this all about, Avi—that's what Shaul wanted to know.

Even as Shaul was agonizing over the sudden appearance of government agents in his doorway, across town in the IRS's Criminal Investigation Division offices, CID chief Ron Saranow was enmeshing himself more deeply than ever in the affairs of the Marcianos. His increasingly chummy ties with the brothers had by now become so open and obvious that many of his colleagues seemed downright embarrassed.

"They're just sucking you along," warned his new boss, a fellow named Fred Nielsen. But Saranow had apparently stopped listening to anyone about the Marcianos. By now he was convinced: They had a job for him at Guess—and not just some rinky-dink managerial job, but maybe the general manager of the whole shooting match. And why not? Whatever Saranow may have felt privately on the matter, to all outward appearances he had certainly given them reason to be impressed with his executive abilities. True, he'd never had much of a role in the Jordache matter, beyond lending an early hand in getting the case off dead center in New York. But hadn't he built a fire under the Bohbot case back here in L.A., where he *was* in charge?

One day in April, Saranow was sitting in his office when one of his top subordinates, a CID branch chief from West Hollywood named Howard, wandered in and began shooting the breeze.

"You know," said Saranow, dropping a name that seemed to fall from his lips more and more of late, "I was just talking with Paul Marciano about something. He's looking for someone to fill a position at Guess. Someone trustworthy and honest. I had a guy in mind, but he's not available. It's too bad."

"What essentially are they looking for?" Howard wanted to know.

Oh, I don't know, said Saranow, someone they could trust and bring on as an executive.

For Saranow the situation must have seemed intensely frustrating. The particular job that the brothers had been talking about was clearly lower down the ladder than what they obviously had in mind for Saranow. Yet here he was, right on the verge of bidding adieu to the IRS and launching a new career with the hottest fashion house in Los Angeles—yet how much executive talent could he really claim to have if he couldn't scrounge up a single live candidate for a middle-level job the brothers wanted to fill?

Fortunately, Howard offered a timely solution. He said, "Well, it sounds interesting, Ron. I might be interested."

Joe, Ralph, and Avi Nakash in their Manhattan showroom. From dirt-poor urchins in Israel they became three of the richest businessmen in New York. (NORA FELLER)

Armand, Georges, Maurice, and Paul Marciano. From the poverty-plagued streets of Marseilles, they became four of the richest businessmen in Beverly Hills. (ALAN LEVENSON/ONYX)

Main Street, Debdu, Morocco, ancestral home of the Marcianos, circa 1915. If there was no invader to rally against, the people would simply fight each other.
(GÉRARD LÉVY COLLECTION, BEN ZVI INSTITUTE, JERUSALEM)

Entrance to Debdu's Jewish quarter. A community split by centuries of desperate, petty feuding between the newcomer Marcianos and a family of older inhabitants, the Cohans.
(GÉRARD LÉVY COLLECTION, BEN ZVI INSTITUTE, JERUSALEM)

Octavio Pena. He might have been a banker from Brazil or a businessman from Alexandria, but he was actually a private eye from New Jersey on the biggest case of his career.
(SHONNAH VALESKA)

Sally Godfrey. An ex-FBI agent with "special skills" in scuba, skydiving, and sex crimes investigations. She worked for Pena, masquerading as "Kelly Grace," a free-lance writer on assignment for Playboy magazine, and eventually wound up a defendant in a racketeering and dirty tricks suit. The case was finally settled out of court, and all claims against Sally were dropped. Here she is shown during more than a week of videotaped depositions in the case.

Paul Marciano. He is shown here being interviewed for a story on the Guess/Jordache fight, which was telecast by ABC's "World News Tonight" on the eve of the Congressional hearings into IRS corruption. In the course of the seven-year struggle, Paul proclaimed fighting the Nakash forces to be his "destiny."
(ABC NEWS)

Marshall Grossman. He was the lead lawyer for the Marcianos, and the Nakashes feared him greatly. His computerized case files seemed to keep him constantly one step ahead of his adversaries. (MARK HANAUER/ONYX)

Top left: *Bruce Dollar. The Kroll Associates official was the main private eye for the Marcianos. He once claimed to have been to over twenty countries in the case, and it was his discovery of alleged tax irregularities in Hong Kong that gave the Marcianos their first real ammunition.* (WILLIAM COUPON)

Top right: *Bart Schwartz. A former prosecutor in the U.S. Attorney's office in New York, he joined Kroll Associates and quickly offered to be helpful by introducing the Marcianos to his successor as chief of the criminal division.* (WILLIAM COUPON)

Led by a charismatic U.S. Attorney, Rudolph Giuliani (see inset), the men and women of the Southern District of New York possessed an esprit de corps unmatched by that of prosecutors anywhere else.

Richard Schauer. The retired appellate court judge was appointed to serve as the tie-breaking seventh member of Guess's board of directors. The Nakashes eventually came to view him as a pawn of the Marcianos. (© BLAKE LITTLE 1990)

Assistant U.S. Attorney Lorna Schofield had become a prosecutor because she wanted to "learn how to be a litigator." Unfortunately, though she wound up handling two of the most complex criminal cases in Southern District history, neither one ever got to trial. (RICHARD LAIRD)

Congressman Douglas Barnard. The Georgia Democrat, chairman of a House government operations subcommittee, is shown here during three days of highly publicized hearings on IRS corruption in Washington, D.C.